S E R I E S

A NavPress Bible study on the book of

1 SAMUEL

NAVPRESS

A MINISTRY OF THE NAVIGATORS

P.O. Box 6000, Colorado Springs, CO 80934

The Navigators is an international Christian organization. Jesus Christ gave His followers the Great Commission to go and make disciples (Matthew 28:19). The aim of The Navigators is to help fulfill that commission by multiplying laborers for Christ in every nation.

NavPress is the publishing ministry of The Navigators. NavPress publications are tools to help Christians grow. Although publications alone cannot make disciples or change lives, they can help believers learn biblical discipleship, and apply what they learn to their lives and ministries.

Most Scripture quotations are from the *Holy Bible: New International Version* (NIV). Copyright © 1973, 1978, 1984, International Bible Society. Used by permission of Zondervan Bible Publishers. Other versions used are the *New American Standard Bible* (NASB), © The Lockman Foundation 1960, 1962, 1963, 1968, 1971, 1972, 1973, 1975, 1977; and the *King James Version* (KJV).

Printed in the United States of America

CONTENTS

ACKNOWLEDGMENTS

The LIFECHANGE series has been produced through the coordinated efforts of a team of Navigator Bible study developers and NavPress editorial staff, along with a nationwide network of fieldtesters.

AUTHOR: WAYNE S. NELSON
SERIES EDITOR: KAREN HINCKLEY

HOW TO USE THIS STUDY

Objectives

Most guides in the LIFECHANGE series of Bible studies cover one book of the Bible. Although the LIFECHANGE guides vary with the books they explore, they share some common goals:

1. To provide you with a firm foundation of understanding and a thirst to return to the book;
2. To teach you by example how to study a book of the Bible without structured guides;
3. To give you all the historical background, word definitions, and explanatory notes you need, so that your only other reference is the Bible;
4. To help you grasp the message of the book as a whole;
5. To teach you how to let God's Word transform you into Christ's image.

Each lesson in this study is designed to take 60 to 90 minutes to complete on your own. The guide is based on the assumption that you are completing one lesson per week, but if time is limited you can do half a lesson per week or whatever amount allows you to be thorough.

Flexibility

LIFECHANGE guides are flexible, allowing you to adjust the quantity and depth of your study to meet your individual needs. The guide offers many optional questions in addition to the regular numbered questions. The optional questions, which appear in the margins of the study pages, include the following:

Optional Application. Nearly all application questions are optional; we hope you will do as many as you can without overcommitting yourself.

For Thought and Discussion. Beginning Bible students should be able to handle these, but even advanced students need to think about them. These questions frequently deal with ethical issues and other biblical principles. They often offer cross-references to spark thought, but the references do not give obvious answers. They are good for group discussions.

For Further Study. These include: a) cross-references that shed light on a topic the book discusses, and b) questions that delve deeper into the passage. You can omit them to shorten a lesson without missing a major point of the passage.

If you are meeting in a group, decide together which optional questions to prepare for each lesson, and how much of the lesson you will cover at the next meeting. Normally, the group leader should make this decision, but you might let each member choose his or her own application questions.

As you grow in your walk with God, you will find the LIFECHANGE guide growing with you—a helpful reference on a topic, a continuing challenge for application, a source of questions for many levels of growth.

Overview and Details

The study begins with an introduction to the book of 1 Samuel. The key to interpretation is context—what is the whole passage or book *about?*—and the key to context is purpose—what is the author's *aim* for the whole work? In lesson one you will lay the foundation for your study of 1 Samuel by asking yourself, "Why did the author (and God) write the book? What did they want to accomplish? What is the book about?"

In lessons two through fifteen you will analyze successive passages of 1 Samuel in detail.

In lesson sixteen you will review 1 Samuel, returning to the big picture to see whether your view of it has changed after closer study. Review will also strengthen your grasp of major issues and give you an idea of how you have grown from your study.

Kinds of Questions

Bible study on your own—without a structured guide—follows a progression. First you observe: What does the passage *say?* Then you interpret: What does the passage *mean?* Lastly you apply: How does this truth *affect* my life?

Some of the "how" and "why" questions will take some creative thinking, even prayer, to answer. Some are opinion questions without clear-cut right answers; these will lend themselves to discussions and side studies.

Don't let your study become an exercise of knowledge alone. Treat the passage as God's Word, and stay in dialogue with Him as you study. Pray, "Lord, what do You want me to see here?" "Father, why is this true?" "Lord, how does this apply to my life?"

It is important that you write down your answers. The act of writing clarifies your thinking and helps you to remember.

Study Aids

A list of reference materials, including a few notes of explanation to help you make good use of them, begins on page 165. This guide is designed to include enough background to let you interpret with just your Bible and the guide. Still, if you want more information on a subject or want to study a book on your own, try the references listed.

Scripture Versions

Unless otherwise indicated, the Bible quotations in this guide are from the New International Version of the Bible. Other versions cited are the New American Standard Bible (NASB) and the King James Version (KJV).

Use any translation you like for study, preferably more than one. A paraphrase such as The Living Bible is not accurate enough for study, but it can be helpful for comparison or devotional reading.

Memorizing and Meditating

A psalmist wrote, "I have hidden your word in my heart that I might not sin against you" (Psalm 119:11). If you write down a verse or passage that challenges or encourages you, and reflect on it often for a week or more, you will find it beginning to affect your motives and actions. We forget quickly what we read once; we remember what we ponder.

When you find a significant verse or passage, you might copy it onto a card to keep with you. Set aside five minutes during each day just to think about what the passage might mean in your life. Recite it over to yourself, exploring its meaning. Then, return to your passage as often as you can during your day, for a brief review. You will soon find it coming to mind spontaneously.

For Group Study

A group of four to ten people allows the richest discussions, but you can adapt this guide for other sized groups. It will suit a wide range of group types, such as home Bible studies, growth groups, youth groups, and businessmen's studies. Both new and experienced Bible students, and new and mature Christians, will benefit from the guide. You can omit or leave for later years any questions you find too easy or too hard.

The guide is intended to lead a group through one lesson per week. However, feel free to split lessons if you want to discuss them more thoroughly. Or, omit some questions in a lesson if preparation or discussion time is limited. You can always return to this guide for personal study later. You will be able to discuss only a few questions at length, so choose some for discussion and others for background. Make time at each discussion for members to ask about anything they didn't understand.

Each lesson in the guide ends with a section called "For the group." These sections give advice on how to focus a discussion, how you might apply the lesson in your group, how you might shorten a lesson, and so on. The group leader should read each "For the group" at least a week ahead so that he or she can tell the group how to prepare for the next lesson.

Each member should prepare for a meeting by writing answers for all of the background and discussion questions to be covered. If the group decides not to take an hour per week for private preparation, then expect to take at least two meetings per lesson to work through the questions. Application will be very difficult, however, without private thought and prayer.

Two reasons for studying in a group are accountability and support. When each member commits in front of the rest to seek growth in an area of life, you can pray with one another, listen jointly for God's guidance, help one another to resist temptation, assure each other that the other's growth matters to you, use the group to practice spiritual principles, and so on. Pray about one another's commitments and needs at most meetings. Spend the first few minutes of each meeting sharing any results from applications prompted by previous lessons. Then discuss new applications toward the end of the meeting. Follow such sharing with prayer for these and other needs.

If you write down each other's applications and prayer requests, you are more likely to remember to pray for them during the week, ask about them at the next meeting, and notice answered prayers. You might want to get a notebook for prayer requests and discussion notes.

Notes taken during discussion will help you to remember, follow up on ideas, stay on the subject, and clarify a total view of an issue. But don't let notetaking keep you from participating. Some groups choose one member at each meeting to take notes. Then someone copies the notes and distributes them at the next meeting. Rotating these tasks can help include people. Some groups have someone take notes on a large pad of paper or erasable marker board (preformed shower wallboard works well), so that everyone can see what has been recorded.

Pages 167-168 list some good sources of counsel for leading group studies. The *Small Group Letter,* published by NavPress, is unique, offering insights from experienced leaders every other month.

INTRODUCTION

The Books of Samuel

Historical setting

The period described in the books of Samuel was only about two or three generations. It began with the birth of Samuel the prophet (about 1105 BC) and extended nearly to the death of David the king (around 970 BC). But this brief period had immense significance for the Israelite nation. It was a time of crisis, of testing, of transition, of failure and judgment, and of faithfulness and blessing.

Israel had come out of the long night of Egyptian slavery as a people mighty only in number. In almost every other respect it was weak and unformed. Only through the grace of God, the labor of Moses, and the raising of a new generation was Israel prepared to make good on its claim to the land of Canaan, which the Lord had promised to Abraham centuries earlier. After Moses, Joshua led the people in conquering and apportioning the land. But following his death the Israelite offensive lost momentum. The people of God became more concerned with settling down than with dispossessing the Canaanite tribes. Thus the Hebrews gradually came to associate with and even resemble those pagan peoples.

The book of Judges documents the disastrous political, social, moral, and religious consequences of Israel's compromise, and God's response to it in judgment and salvation. If during Joshua's leadership the Hebrews knew the blessings of faithfulness to their covenant with God, the time of the judges showed what it meant to live under the covenant's curse for disobedience. The book of 1 Samuel opens toward the end of that time of rebellion and judgment. It tells how the last judge, Samuel, gave way to the first king, Saul. Then, when the reign of Israel's first monarch ended in his defeat and death in battle, God's people seemed destined to perpetual subjugation.

That this did not happen was due, humanly speaking, to two men: Samuel the prophet and David of Bethlehem. These two are the most important figures—after God—in 1 Samuel; one or both of them appear in nearly every chapter of the book.

Timeline—From Samuel to Solomon

(Dates are approximate, based on *The NIV Study Bible*, page 373)

Birth of Samuel (1 Samuel 1:20)	1105 BC
Birth of Saul	1080
Saul anointed to be king (1 Samuel 10:1)	1050
Birth of David	1040
David anointed to be Saul's successor (1 Samuel 16:1-13)	1025
Saul's death and beginning of David's reign over Judah in Hebron (2 Samuel 1:1; 2:1,4,11)	1010
Birth of Solomon (2 Samuel 12:24; 1 Kings 3:7, 11:42)	991
David's death and beginning of Solomon's reign (2 Samuel 5:4-5, 1 Kings 2:10-11)	970
Solomon's death; Israel splits into Israel and Judah (1 Kings 11:41–12:24)	930

In the wider scene of international politics, Canaan was free from external control during the time of Judges and 1 and 2 Samuel. Egypt, which previously had dominated the many independent Canaanite city-states, was prevented from direct involvement there by other concerns. The expansion of the northern powers of Assyria and Babylon, which would later overwhelm Palestine, lay yet in the distant future. Thus, Israel had only to contend with her own internal troubles and nearby neighbors (such as the Philistines), rather than with faraway empires. But even this was enough to threaten Israel's spiritual integrity and political survival.

Literary character

The books of 1 and 2 Samuel were originally one book but were divided around 250 BC when the Hebrew Bible was translated into Greek[1] (they fit on scrolls better that way). Jewish tradition said that Samuel wrote the book, but internal evidence suggests not. Second Samuel extends to the end of David's reign (around 970 BC), when Samuel was long dead. It may be that the author lived shortly after Solomon's death (930 BC). At that time, Israel split into Israel and Judah, a fact to which the books of Samuel refer (see 1 Samuel 11:8, 17:52, 18:16, 27:6; 2 Samuel 5:5, 24:1-9). But the author apparently had access to records of the times (see 2 Samuel 1:18; 1 Chronicles 27:24, 29:29) as well as the help of the Holy Spirit.

Still the title of 1 and 2 Samuel is not wholly inappropriate. The books recount the establishment of monarchy in Israel, and Samuel was the man God used to accomplish this in the way He desired. As you study 1 Samuel, you will observe the crucial role the prophet played in Israel's transition from judges to kings.

Although we may never know for sure when and by whom 1 and 2 Samuel were written, the author's fundamental convictions are clear: God is sovereign, both in history and in the personal lives of individual human beings. And to accomplish His purposes, God works through people, rather than simply through impersonal cultural, social, or economic forces. Thus, the central lesson that 1 and 2 Samuel were designed to teach Israel is that the leader of God's people must be a man after God's heart. The definitive positive example they offer is David (1 Samuel 13:14, Acts 13:22), while the negative counterpart is Saul. The author gives us this truth in a book of history, rather than a treatise, because he knows that God's truth is incarnated in the lives of people, not just expressed in religious or philosophical abstractions.

The books of Samuel belong to the section of the Bible that the Hebrews called the "Former Prophets."[2] This title encompasses Joshua, Judges, Samuel, and Kings. While we are used to thinking of these as historical works, the traditional label is preferable because it points out that the books are prophetic. That is, first of all, the authors were prophets who wrote under God's direction. Second, they were not chronicling events for academicians or historians, but recording God's perspective on happenings in the covenant nation from the entrance into Canaan to the exile into Babylon.

11

The prophet's job was to evaluate how well Israel was living up to its covenant with God and to point out what the people needed to do to get back on track.[3] The prophetic histories, then, recorded what happened with an eye to teaching spiritual lessons critical for God's people.

Modern historians like to call the Former Prophets the "Deuteronomic History." The idea is that Joshua, Judges, Samuel, and Kings must be understood, not as independent works, but as parts of a whole reflection on Israel's history in light of Deuteronomy. This basically reaffirms the traditional outlook: the Former Prophets evaluate and draw lessons from Israel's history in light of the covenant standards stated in Deuteronomy. However, modern scholars go further to note common themes that run through these books. Among the most significant of these are:

1. obedience to God's Word as expressed in the Law of Moses;
2. abhorrence of all idolatrous pagan religion;
3. Israel experiencing either God's blessing or His curse in the promised land according to her obedience to the divine covenant;
4. God's ongoing intervention in His people's life and history, especially through the words and works of the prophets;
5. the ultimate inadequacy of any mere rituals or political institutions to guarantee Israel's survival, prosperity, or (most important of all) spiritual integrity.

Most of these emphases, together with a prediction of Israel's exile from the promised land because of disobedience and unfaithfulness to God, are found explicitly for the first time in the book of Deuteronomy. The revelation to Israel in Deuteronomy reaffirmed and updated for a new generation who were about to enter the promised land the standards that God had already set forth for His people at Sinai (recorded in Exodus). Joshua, Judges, Samuel, and Kings simply compare, explicitly or implicitly, Israel's performance with the Lord's prescriptions.[4]

The four books of the Deuteronomic History (excluding Deuteronomy itself) have an A-B-A-B pattern if we look at the length of time and themes they cover:

Joshua—(one generation) the successful conquest of the land.
Judges—(many generations) the crises of the Israelite confederacy in the land because of sin.
Samuel—(two generations) the successful establishment of the monarchy (David is another Joshua).
Kings—(many generations) from the culmination of the Davidic dream to the collapse of the kingdom because of sin (Zedekiah's end corresponds to Samson's in Judges).

Spiritual legacy

The greatest lasting contribution of this period was not an institution, a document, a tradition, or an idea, but the example of a person: David the son of Jesse from Bethlehem. To this day he is revered by the Jews as one of their two greatest ancient leaders. For Christians, he is the one who, more than any other Old Testament person, prefigured in his experience and character Jesus the Messiah, who was called by those who believed in Him "Son of David" (Matthew 9:27). In fact, God's whole reason for giving Israel a king instead of judges was to take the next step in preparing His people for the Messiah, the true King of Israel.

1. *The NIV Study Bible*, edited by Kenneth Barker (Grand Rapids, Michigan: Zondervan Corporation, 1985), page 371.
2. The Jews have traditionally divided the Old Testament Scriptures into three categories: Law, Prophets, and Writings. Law embraces the first five books (Genesis through Deuteronomy). The Prophets are divided between the "Former" and the "Latter" Prophets. The Latter Prophets are the books we think of as prophetic (Isaiah through Malachi, minus Daniel). The Writings comprise the books we consider poetic (Job, Psalms, Proverbs, Ecclesiastes, the Song of Songs) plus 1 and 2 Chronicles, Ruth, Ezra, Nehemiah, Esther, and Daniel.
3. The Former Prophets emphasize predictive prophecy less than prophecy that evaluates and exhorts.
4. Many of the scholars who talk about the Deuteronomic History also have highly speculative theories about the authors and dates of the books. So, while their approach is useful in some ways, we will focus on interpreting Scripture in light of Scripture rather than according to modern scholarship or ancient tradition.

OVERVIEW

It is much easier to study a book passage by passage after you have first examined it as a whole. The most important message of a narrative book like 1 Samuel is often in the whole, not the parts. So, begin your study of 1 Samuel by reading through it according to the following schedule:

first reading—chapters 1-7
second reading—chapters 8-15
third reading—chapters 16-20
fourth reading—chapters 21-31

In this first time through the book, don't stop to untangle all the details or reflect on interesting passages. Simply try to form a first impression of what the book is about. Write answers to questions 1 through 3 as you complete each section. Ask the Lord to sharpen your attention and show you what is important as you read.

Study Skill—Identifying Major Divisions
When you begin studying a long book like 1 Samuel, it is helpful to notice major divisions in the narrative. This awareness will help you keep the whole book in focus and appreciate how it develops its message. The major divisions are often indicated by a particularly significant event, the first appearance of an important individual or group, or
(continued on page 16)

For Further Study:
The book of Judges gives crucial background to the events of 1 Samuel. Read Judges 1:1-3:6 (which describes the overall pattern of events during the period of the judges), 6:1-6 (which explains the severity of the foreign oppression Israel suffered), and 19:1-20:48 (which recounts the nation's internal difficulties).

(continued from page 15)
the introduction of a new subject or theme. Each part of the book contributes to the meaning of the whole and so should never be isolated from it, but observing the parts can help you see how they add up to the whole message.

1. For each of the four major parts of 1 Samuel, identify the three or four most important persons and events.

chapters 1-7 (persons) _____

_____

(events) _____

_____

_____

_____

chapters 8-15 (persons) _____

_____

(events) _____

_____

_____

_____

chapters 16-20 (persons) _____

_____

(events) _____

_____

_____

_____

chapters 21-31 (persons) _____

_____

(events) _____

_____

_____

_____

For Thought and Discussion: What is the mood of 1 Samuel? Is it generally upbeat, pessimistic, or mixed? Why do you see it like this?

2. For each of these major sections, describe the political condition of Israel.

chapters 1-7 _____

_____

chapters 8-15 _____

_____

chapters 16-20 _____

_____

chapters 21-31 _____

_____

3. Similarly, for each section, summarize the spiritual state of the nation—its leaders and the Israelites as a whole.

chapters 1-7 _____

_____

chapters 8-15 _____

_____

chapters 16-20 _____

_____

chapters 21-31 _____

_____

4. What relationship do you see between Israel's political fortunes and spiritual state?

_____

_____

17

For Thought and Discussion: Are there any elements in the book that you have difficulty understanding or accepting? What are they, and why?

For Thought and Discussion: How is the type of history you find in 1 Samuel different from modern historical books?

_____

_____

_____

5. a. Which group poses the most serious threat to Israel in the opening chapters of 1 Samuel, and which group in its closing chapters?

opening _____

closing _____

  b. What do you think is the significance of this?

_____

_____

_____

_____

6. What role does God's miraculous intervention play in the narrative?

_____

_____

_____

_____

Study Skill—Themes

The most important purpose of an overview is to make some initial decisions on what the book is about. Ideas that recur over and over are a clue to the book's themes. A contrast between two individuals is another clue. A third is conflict between two individuals, between two groups, between an individual and his circumstances, or within an individual. A fourth clue is how things change over the course of the book, and why.

   You can change your mind about themes later on, but always form some preliminary opinions by reading through the book in an overview.

7. What would you say 1 Samuel as a whole is about? What are its main themes, or the main message the author means to convey?

_____

_____

_____

_____

_____

_____

Study Skill—Outlines
When you've identified the main divisions of a book, try giving each a title or summarizing its contents. Let your titles or summaries reflect the main theme(s) of the book.

As you study 1 Samuel, think about and evaluate these two outlines of the book:

Outline A
Part 1 (1 Samuel 1-12): In the context of judgment upon the priestly family of Eli, God raises up a leader for His people in the person of Samuel.

Part 2 (1 Samuel 13-31): In the context of judgment upon the royal family of Saul, God raises up a leader for His people in the person of David.

Outline B[1]
  I. Historical setting for the establishment of kingship in Israel (1 Samuel 1-7).
 II. The kingship established under the guidance of Samuel the prophet (1 Samuel 8-12).
III. Saul's kingship fails (1 Samuel 13-15).
 IV. Saul's reign deteriorates; David rises to the throne (1 Samuel 16:1-2 Samuel 5:5).
  V. David's kingship in its accomplishments and glory (2 Samuel 5:6-9:12).
 VI. David's kingship in its weaknesses and failures (2 Samuel 10-20).
VII. Final reflections on David's reign (2 Samuel 21-24).

19

8. Your overview may have suggested issues you want to explore and questions you want to answer as you study in more depth. If so, jot them down to serve as personal objectives for the rest of your study. What do you want to understand better by the time you are finished?

_____

_____

_____

_____

_____

_____

Study Skill—Application

Second Timothy 3:16-17 says, "All Scripture . . . is useful for teaching, rebuking, correcting and training in righteousness, so that the man of God may be thoroughly equipped for every good work." Paul also writes, "For everything that was written in the past was written to teach us, so that through endurance and the encouragement of the Scriptures we might have hope" (Romans 15:4), and "These things happened to them as examples and were written down as warnings for us" (1 Corinthians 10:11). Therefore, when you study 1 Samuel, you should keep asking yourself, "What difference should this passage make in my life? How should it make me want to think or act? How does it encourage, warn, correct, or set me an example?"

Application will require time, thought, prayer, and perhaps even discussion with another person. You may sometimes find it more productive to concentrate on one application, giving it careful thought and prayer, than to list several potential applications without really reflecting on them or committing yourself to them. At other times, you may want to list many implications that a passage has for your life. Then you can choose one of these to act or meditate upon.

9. Are there any people or experiences in 1 Samuel with which you can identify personally? If so, who or what are they?

_____

_____

_____

_____

_____

_____

_____

10. In your first reading, did you find any truths that are relevant to your life? If so, was there anything you would like to commit to memory, pray about, or act on? Write down your plans.

_____

_____

_____

_____

_____

_____

For the group

This "For the group" section and the ones in later lessons are intended to suggest ways of structuring your discussions. Feel free to select what suits your group. The main goals of this lesson are to get to know the book of 1 Samuel and the people with whom you are going to study it. If you have never done a LIFECHANGE study before, you might want to take one meeting to do the "warm-up" below and discuss the "How to Use This Study" section on pages 5-8, and a second meeting to discuss lesson one. This will also give the group more time to read the Introduction on pages 9-13, read all of 1 Samuel, and answer the questions in lesson one.

Worship. Some groups like to begin with prayer and/or singing. Some share requests for prayer at the beginning but leave the actual prayer until after the study. Others prefer just to chat and have refreshments for awhile, then open the study with a brief prayer for the Holy Spirit's guidance, and leave worship and prayer until the end.

Warm-up. The beginning of a new study is a good time to lay a foundation for honest sharing of ideas, to get comfortable with each other, and to encourage a sense of common purpose. One way to establish common ground is to talk about what each person hopes to get out of your study of 1 Samuel, and out of any prayer, singing, sharing, outreach, or anything else you might do together. You can also share what you hope to give as well as get. If you have someone write down each member's hopes and expectations, then you can look back at these goals later to see if they are being met. Goal-setting at the beginning can also help you avoid confusion when one person thinks the main point of the group is to learn the Scripture, while another thinks it is to support each other in daily Christian life, and another thinks prayer or outreach is the chief business.

How to use this study. Advise group members to read the "How to Use This Study" section on pages 5-8 if they have not already done so. You might go over important points that you think the group should especially notice. For example, point out the optional questions in the margins. These are available as group discussion questions, ideas for application, and suggestions for further study. It is unlikely that anyone will have the time or desire to answer all the optional questions and do all the applications. A person might do one "Optional Application" for any given lesson. You might choose one or two "For Thought and Discussion" questions for your group discussion, or you might spend all your time on the numbered questions. If someone wants to write answers to the optional questions, suggest that he use a separate notebook. It will also be helpful for discussion notes, prayer requests, answers to prayers, application plans, and so on.

Invite everyone to ask questions about the "How to Use This Study" section.

Overview. Ideally, everyone should have read the whole book of 1 Samuel and the Introduction before you meet together. However, some may not have done so, and others may not retain much of what they read quickly. So, ask a few questions to draw out the main points of the Introduction, such as:

1. What do you remember of Israel's history up to the point where 1 Samuel picks it up?
2. What is "prophetic history"? How is it helpful for you to know that 1 Samuel is a prophetic book?
3. What is a "covenant"? What were the basic terms of the covenant between God and Israel?

You may have to explain that 1 Samuel is not necessarily prophetic in the sense of foretelling the future, but it is prophetic in the sense of interpreting history from a prophet's perspective. That is, the story is told with a focus on God and His covenant with His people. (Page 107 gives a simple definition of the word *covenant*.)

Now go on to the questions in lesson one. You might find it helpful to divide a blackboard or a large piece of paper into four sections for the four sections of the book. In each section, write down the major persons and events, and the political and spiritual states of the nation (questions 1 through 3). With this in front of you discuss questions 4 through 7. The Introduction suggests some themes of the book, but you may find better ways of expressing them.

Take a few minutes to look at the outlines on page 19 together. If you have study Bibles or commentaries, compare the outlines they give. What do you find helpful in each outline?

Let everyone share questions he or she has about the book. Save these to answer as you study in detail, and come back to them at the end to see if you have answered all of them.

Don't spend a lot of time on application in this lesson. Later lessons will attempt to guide those who are unsure how to apply Scripture to their lives. However, do share any ways you were able to identify with the characters and incidents in the story, and any ways you found the book relevant to

23

your lives. Questions 9 and 10 should help you get to know each other better and give everyone something to think about during the week.

Wrap-up. Briefly tell the group what to expect in lesson two. Whet everyone's appetite, and ask the group to think about any optional questions that you plan to discuss.

Worship. Many groups like to end with singing and/or prayer. This can include songs or prayers that respond to what you've learned in Bible study, or prayers for specific needs of group members. Some people are shy about sharing personal needs or praying aloud in groups, especially before they know the other people well. If this is true of your group, then a song and/or some silent prayer and a short closing prayer spoken by the leader might be an appropriate ending.

1. Adapted from *The NIV Study Bible*, pages 373-374.

1 SAMUEL 1:1-2:36

New Birth, New Beginning

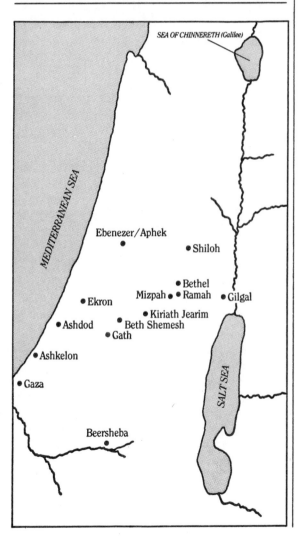

For Further Study:
Barrenness was a common source of grief to women in the ancient east. Read about the feelings and actions of other barren women (Genesis 16:1-16, 18:10-15, 30:1-24). Why did God permit the barrenness in each case, and how was it overcome?

For Thought and Discussion: Whom do you think the author wished to emphasize as the most important individual in 1:1-2:36? How does he underscore this person's significance?

For a book that gives much attention to political and military affairs, these opening chapters are surprising. Rather than a rehearsal of Israel's national crisis, we find the private anguish of one woman. Yet private struggles have public import repeatedly in the Scriptures. Read all of 1:1-2:36 before beginning the questions in this lesson. Ask the Lord to speak to you in your situation through the story of Hannah and Eli.

Samuel's birth (1:1-2:11)

1. Describe Hannah's plight (1:1-7).

_____

_____

_____

_____

Ramathaim (1:1). This seems to be another name for Ramah (1:19, 2:11). It is probably the Ramah in Benjamin about five miles north of Jerusalem. For places named in chapters 1-7, see the map on page 25.

Ephraimite (1:1). Since his son became a priest, Elkanah was probably a Levite whose family belonged to the clans that had been allotted towns in Ephraim (Joshua 21:20-21).[1]

Two wives (1:2). Having more than one wife at once was never the rule in the ancient world, and only kings had large harems. Yet several Old Testament figures, such as Abraham and Jacob, had more than one wife. The reasons for polygamy were more cultural and economic than erotic. When organized government was weak or nonexistent and each family had to care for itself, a large number of children was often considered a necessity. Thus when one wife failed to bear children for her husband, he might take another also (Genesis 16:1-4, 25:1-4). Even in the case of monarchs, marriages were often more a means of sealing an alliance than any-

26

thing else (1 Kings 3:1). So polygamy, while never God's purpose for the human race, should not be regarded in itself as a sign of immorality.

Year after year (1:3). Every Israelite male was required to attend festivals at the central sanctuary three times a year (Deuteronomy 16:16-17). Elkanah probably brought his wives to the Feast of Tabernacles, when the nation celebrated God's blessing on the year's fertility of crops and herds (Deuteronomy 16:13-15). This would have been an especially sad time for a barren woman.

The LORD Almighty (1:3). "The LORD of hosts" in KJV, NASB. "Hosts" are armies of men or angels (the word is also used of the sun, moon, and stars). The books of Samuel emphasize that the Lord is the commander of both the armies of Israel and the armies of heaven.

Temple (1:9). Solomon did not build a permanent structure for the Lord's worship until about a century later (1 Kings 6:1). Before this, the tabernacle—an elaborate royal tent—served as the nation's sanctuary. After Israel settled in Canaan, the tabernacle was apparently erected at Shiloh more or less permanently until the time of David. In these circumstances, it may have become "part of a larger, more permanent building complex to which the term 'temple' could legitimately be applied."[2] (Notice the mention of sleeping quarters and doors in 3:2,15.)

No razor (1:11). In dedicating her future son to the Lord, Hannah placed him under a Nazirite vow (like Samson in Judges 13:2-5). This vow was a way of expressing one's devotion or gratitude to the Lord, but it normally involved only a limited period of time rather than one's whole life (Numbers 6:1-21, Acts 21:20-26).

2. What attitudes toward her situation and the Lord does Hannah show in 1:9-11,15-16?

   her situation _____

_____

For Thought and Discussion: What do you think was behind Hannah's desire to bear a child? Consider 1:6,11.

For Thought and Discussion: Eli thought Hannah was drunk at the tabernacle (1:13). What does this tell you about the moral condition of Israel?

For Thought and Discussion: Samuel's name sounds like the Hebrew for "heard of God." How is this relevant to Samuel's function in Israel?

_____

_____

the Lord _____

_____

_____

_____

3. In light of 2:12-17 and 3:12-13, what irony do you see in the fact that Eli assumed that Hannah was drunk (1:12-14)?

_____

_____

_____

_____

_____

Study Skill—Observation

Careful and observant reading is crucial to correctly interpreting and applying the Scriptures. (Reading a passage in several translations can help you notice things you might otherwise have missed.) The clues that enable you to draw accurate conclusions are often details. For example, if you miss the details of Eli's family in 2:12-17 and 3:12-13, you might miss the irony of his accusation against Hannah. Also, in order to decide whether Hannah's vow in 1:11 was righteous or manipulative, you need to take into account the whole story, as well as what the Scripture says elsewhere about vows and prayer.

Weaned (1:22). It was normal to nurse children for three years or more, since animal's milk could not be refrigerated for children to drink.[3]

4. Consider Hannah's prayer in 1:11 and her subsequent actions in 1:20-2:11. Do you think Hannah sought primarily a son to silence Peninnah or a way to serve the Lord? Why do you think so?

_____

_____

_____

_____

_____

_____

5. In your judgment, is Hannah's prayer in 1:11 meant to be a positive or negative example for us today, or no example at all? Why?

_____

_____

_____

_____

_____

6. What was the result for Hannah of her prayer, vow, and gift to God (2:18-21)?

_____

_____

_____

_____

_____

7. Psalms of praise frame the beginning and end of the books of Samuel (1 Samuel 2:1-10, 2 Samuel 22:1-51). Together they express the theology of the work in song form. What does Hannah declare about God in 2:1-10? Write

Optional Application: Hannah wanted to have something she could consecrate entirely to the Lord. Does this desire affect your prayer life? Should it? This week, try to think of something you can ask of the Lord in order to dedicate it to Him.

For Further Study: The book of Ruth also emphasizes the role of women and children in Israel's history and God's blessings. It also gives a glimpse of everyday life a few decades before Samuel's birth.

29

For Further Study:
Compare 1 Samuel
2:1-10 to Luke
1:46-55. What is sim-
ilar about the causes
and contents of each
song? Do you think
Mary was imitating
Hannah on purpose?
Why or why not?

For Further Study:
At least six other chil-
dren in the Bible are
conceived by special
acts of God: Isaac,
Jacob and Esau, Sam-
son, John the Baptist,
and Jesus. Study the
circumstances sur-
rounding each birth.
What might be the
point of this pattern?

For Further Study:
How does 1 Samuel
1:1-2:10 illustrate
Ephesians 3:20?

**For Thought and
Discussion:** What
does it mean to call
God a "Rock" (2:2)?

down as many observations about Him as you
can find.

_____

_____

_____

_____

_____

_____

_____

_____

_____

_____

8. How are the truths in 2:1-11 relevant to . . .

the rest of 1 Samuel? _____

_____

_____

_____

_____

your life personally? _____

_____

_____

_____

_____

Eli's family (2:12-36)

Practice of the priests (2:13). It was right to have a
way to get a fair portion of fellowship offerings
for the priests (Leviticus 7:28-36), but 1 Samuel
2:15-16 shows an abuse of a fair practice. The

Law specified boiled meat for the priests (Numbers 6:19-20). Roasting was not forbidden, but it was unreasonable for Eli's sons to refuse boiled meat (1 Samuel 2:15). Furthermore, the Law required that the Lord's portion be burned first before the priests got their share, but Eli's sons wanted theirs first (1 Samuel 2:15-16). Finally, they were threatening force (1 Samuel 2:16), but the gift to them was supposed to be voluntary.

9. Besides the personal and family experiences of Hannah, 1:1-2:36 presents a portrait of the priestly family of Eli. What contrasts do you observe between these two families?

_____

_____

_____

_____

_____

10. How would you summarize the message of the man of God to Eli (2:27-36)?

_____

_____

_____

_____

_____

_____

Optional Application: Are you guilty of taking for granted and abusing your spiritual privileges in any ways, as Eli's sons did?

For Thought and Discussion: What might be the significance of the way 1 Samuel begins with a look at two contrasting family situations? What point might the author be making about families and Israel's crisis?

For Thought and Discussion: What can the cases of Hannah's and Eli's sons teach us about a parent's responsibility for the spiritual nurture of children? (See also 8:1-5.) How might modern parents avoid Eli's rebuke?

Man of God (2:27). A way of referring to a prophet.

Father's house (2:27). The descendants of Aaron (see the box on page 36).

Raise up for myself a faithful priest (2:35). Zadok, who became a priest under David and high

31

For Thought and Discussion: God's judgment upon Eli's family canceled a promise He had made previously (2:30). How is the fulfillment of God's promises related to man's performance?

priest under Solomon (2 Samuel 8:17, 1 Kings 2:35), came from a different line than Eli. Zadok's descendants were the high priests from then until about 170 BC.

11. Why do you think the story of how kingship in Israel was established begins with the birth and dedication of Samuel and the curse upon Eli's house?

_____

_____

_____

_____

_____

Study Skill—Interpreting Old Testament Narratives

A narrative is a story. When we read a biblical narrative, we are reading part of the true story about God as He revealed Himself to people over centuries. Here are some principles for interpreting any biblical narrative, particularly Old Testament ones:

1. Not every episode in Israel's history is meant to teach an individual moral lesson. Sometimes a story is significant only as part of the whole history of God's dealings with Israel.

2. Narratives record what happened, not necessarily what ought to happen every time. So again, a particular story may not have its own moral. (For example, the fact that Hannah made a vow to dedicate Samuel may not be a timeless model for barren women.)

3. Not every detail of a narrative has deep significance. (The exact way Eli's sons exploited worshipers probably doesn't.) The point may be in the overall message. However, the point may not be clear until we carefully observe many details. (By comparing the sons' practices to the laws in Leviticus and

(continued on page 33)

(continued from page 32)

Deuteronomy, we can see that their behavior violated not just general courtesy but express commands of God.)

4. Narratives often teach by clearly implying something without actually stating it. (We may infer that 2:18-21 is meant to imply that the Lord rewarded Hannah for her generous gift of her son.) However, we should be wary of teachers who see "hidden" meanings that other Christians do not see.

5. A narrative will never imply something that another passage of Scripture explicitly contradicts or forbids. We use the plain teaching portions of Scripture to evaluate what happens in the narrative portions.

6. "*All* narratives are selective and incomplete. Not all the relevant details are always given (see John 21:25). What does appear in the narrative is everything that the inspired author thought important for us to know." (We must be content with our curiosity unsatisfied about details of Samuel's, Saul's, David's, and others' lives that the Scripture does not give.)

7. "Narratives are not written to answer all our theological questions. They have particular, specific, limited purposes and deal with certain issues, leaving others to be dealt with elsewhere in other ways." (The text doesn't address whether Eli was "saved" or "damned," and we shouldn't speculate.)

8. God is the main character (the hero) of all biblical narratives. The human beings are always secondary characters in a story about what God did.[4]

Optional Application: How would you feel if you gave your only son to be raised by a man with Eli's record as a father? What does this say about Hannah's faith in God? How can you show similar faith in something God wants you to do?

Your response

12. What do you think is the main point we are intended to get from 1:1-2:36?

_____

_____

_____

_____

_____

13. How is this truth relevant to your life? Or, what other truth from this passage seems most relevant to you right now?

_____

_____

_____

_____

_____

14. How would you like this truth to affect your habits, outlook, priorities, and actions?

_____

_____

_____

_____

_____

15. What action can you take to begin letting this happen, with God's help?

_____

_____

_____

_____

_____

16. If you have any questions about anything in 1:1–2:36, write them down so that you can pursue answers.

_____

_____

_____

For the group

Worship.

Warm-up. People often come to Bible study groups with their minds still full of the day's busyness. Beginning with worship can help people change mental gears to focus on God. One way to help them open up to each other and start thinking about the issues of the study is to ask a question about their lives that relates to the topic at hand. In this lesson you might ask, "What is one thing you are praying fervently for?" Encourage everyone to respond aloud, but give everyone the freedom to pass.

Read aloud. It is usually helpful to have someone read the whole passage aloud before you start discussing it. This refreshes everyone's memory, sets the tone of the discussion, and may even let people notice details they hadn't seen before. With long narrative passages as in 1 Samuel, it can be fun to assign the parts of the narrator and the various characters to different readers. Ask each to read with the tone of voice he or she thinks Hannah, Eli, etc. would have used.

Summarize. Before you plunge into the details of this episode, ask someone to summarize what happens in 1:1-2:36.

Questions. The lessons in this study cover two or three chapters at a time. So, you may not be able to discuss every question with equal depth. If group members have prepared their answers ahead of time, it may not be necessary to read answers to all of the simple observation questions. The leader should choose ahead of time those numbered and marginal questions that seem to offer fruitful discussions. Even if you have time to delve into only two or three meaty interpretation questions, you will have spent your time well.

Always allow at least ten minutes to discuss how each of you plans to apply the passage to your lives. In later lessons you will find more guidance on applying Old Testament narratives and Scripture in general. Encourage each person to tell the group, "The part of this passage that applies to my life is . . . and what I want to do about it is. . . ."

Ask if anyone in the group has questions about the passage or the lesson. For instance, the Study Skill on page 32 may raise some questions. If someone has a question, ask the group to answer it. If the group can't, you can either answer it yourself or suggest a source where the person might find an answer. It is always a good idea to help group members learn to do things for themselves rather than rely on the leader, but this is not always possible.

Summarize. Before your discussion, you summarized what happened in the passage. After your discussion, summarize the point you think the passage makes. Why does 1 Samuel begin with the story of Samuel's birth and the prophecy against Eli's family? What does this passage contribute to the book as a whole? What did you learn from the passage that is relevant to your lives?

Wrap-up. Remind the group to look back at the Study Skill on page 32 as they prepare lesson three.

Prayer. Thank God for working through one faithful woman to raise up a leader in Israel's time of need. Praise Him for His holy justice in dealing with wicked priests and for His holy mercy in answering a barren woman's cry. Praise Him that even when the nation was in social, political, and moral decay, He was in control and taking steps to see right and blessing prevail. Ask Him to hear the fervent requests each of you has been praying, and to take action both in your personal lives and in the lives of His whole people.

The Aaronic Priesthood

Priests and sacrifices play a major role in 1 Samuel, so you should know something about Israel's priestly system.

While God told His people that they were to be to Him "a kingdom of priests and a holy nation" (Exodus 19:5-6), He selected one tribe within Israel to serve as mediators between Him

(continued on page 37)

(continued from page 36)
and the rest. That tribe was Levi (Exodus 32:26-29), and from it one family, descended from Aaron, was to perform the priestly functions (Exodus 27:20–28:4). While this was a great privilege, it also exposed those who served as priests to great danger. In fact, no sooner had Aaron and his sons been installed as priests, than two of his offspring were consumed by fire for trying to offer to the Lord something He had not commanded (Leviticus 10:1-3).

The priests continued to serve throughout Israel's history, but they seldom provided effective spiritual leadership or hindered religious apostasy. (One exception is Jehoiada, 2 Kings 11:1-20.) God wiped out the family of Eli for its failures and transferred the priesthood to the descendants of Aaron through Zadok (1 Kings 2:26-27).

1. *The NIV Study Bible*, page 375.
2. *The NIV Study Bible*, page 375.
3. *The NIV Study Bible*, page 376.
4. Gordon Fee and Douglas Stuart, *How to Read the Bible for All Its Worth* (Grand Rapids, Michigan: Zondervan Corporation, 1982), pages 74-75, 78.

1 SAMUEL 3:1-4:22

Departing Glory

Before the new order represented by Samuel can be inaugurated, the old must be put away. As Samuel grows physically and spiritually, God reiterates through him His intention to judge Eli's family. In 1 Samuel 3:1-4:22, we see the terrible beginning of that judgment. Read this passage before beginning the questions below.

Samuel's call (3:1-21)

The lamp of God (3:3). The golden lampstand that stood in the Holy Place. It was against the Law for the priests to allow the lamp to go out before morning (Leviticus 24:1-4).

1. How does 3:1-21 describe Samuel's spiritual character and growth (3:1,7,19-21)?

_____

_____

_____

_____

_____

_____

For Thought and Discussion: On what did Samuel's success as a prophet and leader of Israel depend (2:19-21)? How is this relevant to leaders today? How is it relevant to you?

Optional Application: How can you show yourself to be as ready as Samuel was to receive God's word?

For Thought and Discussion: God's word in 2:27-36 and 3:11-14 is stern. Is God's word that we proclaim today ever like that? Why or why not?

For Further Study: a. Old Testament prophecies of judgment were not necessarily intended to make their audiences pessimistic. What were the purposes of the prophecies in 1 Kings 21:17-24 and Jeremiah 18:5-12?
b. How does this apply to the prophecies against Eli's house? To warnings God gives today?

2. To "know" someone in Hebrew signified intimate, direct relationship. In what sense did Samuel "know" the Lord after his call in a way he didn't before it (3:7)?

_____

_____

_____

_____

_____

From Dan to Beersheba (3:20). A way of referring to the whole land and its people. Dan was in the far north of the country, and Beersheba in the far south.

3. How does God's first revelation to Samuel (3:11-14) compare to what He had already revealed through the man of God (2:27-36)?

_____

_____

_____

4. Why do you think God twice warned Eli concerning the judgment that was impending against his family? What does this say about God?

_____

_____

_____

_____

_____

5. What effect do you suppose this message had on Samuel?

_____

40

_____

_____

_____

_____

6. To what degree was Eli responsible for his sons' conduct (2:22-25, 3:13)?

_____

_____

_____

_____

_____

Optional Application: a. How do you think God wanted Eli to respond to His warnings?

b. Has God given you any words you should respond to? If so, how?

Study Skill—Interpreting Narratives
Principle number 1 on page 32 says that not every episode in a narrative is meant to teach an individual moral lesson. To what extent is this true of 3:1-21? We can draw personal lessons about Samuel's attentiveness and Eli's passive, almost fatalistic, acceptance of God's word, but isn't the real point of the chapter how God raised up a particular servant in a particular situation? The main "moral" of chapter 3 is a theme of the book as a whole: God is in control at every stage, shaping people and events for His purposes. Decide for yourself to what extent principle number 1 applies to later episodes of 1 Samuel.

The ark is captured (4:1-22)

Philistines (4:1). They apparently came from the west, the Mediterranean, sometime between 1500 and 1200 BC, and settled on the southern coastal plain of the promised land. Their five major cities (Ashdod, Gaza, Gath, Ashkelon, and Ekron) formed a strong political-military coalition. They were also technologically superior to Israel (1 Samuel 13:19-22).

Their political, military, and technological strength made them a real threat to the Hebrew tribes.

The ark of the LORD's covenant (4:3). A box or chest, on the top of which were the figures of two angels (Exodus 25:10-22). The ark contained the stone tablets on which the Ten Commandments were inscribed, along with certain other objects from the time of Israel's wilderness wanderings. It was considered the most sacred of all of the tabernacle's furnishings and symbolized God's presence in the midst of His people.

    The use of the ark in the overthrow of Jericho (Joshua 6:2-21) may have encouraged Israel to try to employ it against the Philistines. Pagans believed that a god was identified with the symbol of his presence, and that his help could automatically be secured by manipulating his symbol.[1]

7. According to Deuteronomy 28:15,25, for what reasons did the Lord allow Israel to be defeated by the Philistines (1 Samuel 4:2)?

8. In bringing the ark against the Philistines (4:2-4), was Israel demonstrating true faith in the Lord? Why or why not?

For Thought and Discussion: Israel often experienced military defeats in times of spiritual decay. In the Christian life, does unfaithfulness to God always, sometimes, or never lead to visible problems? What is your experience?

9. a. How did the Philistines react to the news that the ark was coming into battle (4:5-9)?

_____

_____

_____

b. What did they apparently know about the God of Israel?

_____

_____

_____

c. How do you think their victory over Israel affected their opinion about the Lord?

_____

_____

_____

d. The Lord sent the plagues on Egypt in order to prove He was the mightiest God (Exodus 7:1-5). He was usually very concerned to demonstrate His sovereignty to the pagans

43

For Thought and Discussion: The birth of a child is normally a joyous occasion. How do the births of Samuel and of Eli's grandson compare in this respect, and why?

For Further Study: Why does God's glory depart from Israel in Ezekiel 10:3-11:25? How does this compare to the situation in 1 Samuel 4, and why?

Israel met (Joshua 4:23-24). Why, then, did He let the Philistines defeat Israel when His ark was present?

_____

_____

_____

_____

_____

10. Why were Eli and his daughter-in-law more horrified about the ark's capture than about the death of his sons and her husband (4:12-22)?

_____

_____

_____

_____

Your response

Study Skill—Applying Old Testament Narratives

Keep the following five guidelines in mind when you try to apply Old Testament narratives to yourself:

1. What people do in narratives is not necessarily a good example to us. Frequently it is just the opposite (4:3-4 is an instance of this).

2. Most of the characters in narratives are far from perfect, and so are their actions. This is true of obvious sinners like Eli and even great men like David. Thus, we should not try to copy everything even David does. We should let the rest of Scripture, especially the New Testament, guide us in drawing lessons for application.

3. We are not always told at the end of a

(continued on page 45)

(continued from page 44)
narrative whether what happened was good
or bad. (Was it good or bad that the ark was
captured?) We are expected to be able to
decide that on tne basis of what God has
said directly elsewhere in the Scriptures.

4. In every case, God is speaking to and
dealing with a particular person (such as
Samuel, Eli, Saul, or David). We should not
think we are supposed to do everything He
tells someone in the narrative to do. (For
instance, since He commanded different tactics in almost every one of Israel's battles, we
can't assume that we should adopt one or
another of those tactics for one of our battles. Samuel's instructions to Saul in chapters
13 and 15 are also specific to those situations.) Instead of looking for tactics to copy,
we should focus on God's character, His
aims, and the variety of His methods. We
should pray for discernment from the Holy
Spirit and uncoerced confirmation from other
Christians before we apply a specific command (such as to wait, go forward, or make
peace) to ourselves.

5. If God's Word illustrates a principle
that the New Testament would uphold, then
we can apply the principle to *genuinely com-
parable* situations in our own lives. Our task
is to discern the principle accurately and
make sure that our situations are truly com-
parable. This is not always easy, and it always
requires wisdom from the Holy Spirit and guidance from the New Testament. Discussion
with other discerning Christians also helps
guard against error.[2]

11. What would you say is the main point God
means us to get from 3:1-4:22?

_____

_____

_____

_____

12. What one truth from these chapters would you
like to take to heart and apply?

_____

_____

_____

_____

_____

13. How do you fall short or need to grow in this
area? How would you like this truth to affect
your thoughts and actions?

_____

_____

_____

_____

_____

14. What steps can you take along these lines
during the coming week?

_____

_____

_____

_____

_____

15. Write down any questions you have about
3:1–4:22.

_____

_____

_____

_____

For the group

Warm-up. Ask, "What would you do if God warned you that your descendants would all suffer because of your failure as a parent?" This is a shocking question, but it may help the group feel for Eli.

Read aloud and summarize.

Questions. Refer to the three Study Skills in this lesson and the two in lesson two as you discuss the questions in this lesson. Choose a few meaty discussion questions, and be sure to allow plenty of time for personal application.

Prayer. Thank God for making His will known through prophets like Samuel. Thank Him for having everything under control, even when His people are foolish and willful. Ask Him to make you as attentive to Him as Samuel, and to keep you from trying to manipulate Him as Israel did.

1. *The NIV Study Bible*, page 380.
2. Fee and Stuart, page 78.

1 SAMUEL 5:1-7:17

The Lord Against the Philistines

The ark of the covenant had shown itself to be anything but a lucky charm that Israel could manipulate at will. Brought into battle by the hard-pressed Hebrew tribes, this time it only worked against them. But the Philistines' exultation upon capturing Israel's most sacred object was short-lived. Read 5:1-7:17.

The ark in Philistia (5:1-12)

Ashdod . . . Gath . . . Ekron (5:1,8,10). Find these Philistine cities on the map on page 25.

Dagon (5:2). Probably the grain god and principle deity of the middle Euphrates region (upriver from Babylon). His worship spread to Canaan, and he became the Philistines' main god (Judges 16:21,23,26; 1 Chronicles 10:10). Canaanite mythology called Dagon the son (or brother) of El and the father of Baal.[1]

To this day (5:5). The time when 1 and 2 Samuel were written.

1. How did the Philistines treat the ark at first (5:1-2)?

_____

_____

For Thought and Discussion: What do you think the Philistines thought the capture of the ark proved? What did it really prove?

_____

_____

2. They were no doubt thrilled to have captured the ark. What caused them to change their opinion about it (5:3-12)?

_____

_____

_____

_____

_____

3. What do you think God taught Israel and Philistia by allowing the ark to be captured, then doing what 5:3-4,6,9,11-12 describes?

_____

_____

_____

_____

_____

In the ancient world, the capture of an enemy's sacred objects was considered momentous. Daniel 1:1-2 recounts how Nebuchadnezzar took vessels from the Temple at Jerusalem and placed them in the temple of his god in Babylonia. Theoretically, the power of the god whose objects had been captured would be available to the victors. By contrast, God had commanded Israel not to incorporate any pagan customs or objects of worship into its religion (Exodus 23:23-24,32-33; 34:11-17).

The ark returned (6:1-7:1)

4. How could the Philistines tell that the ark's return to Israel was sovereignly directed by the Lord (6:1-12)?

_____

_____

_____

_____

_____

Study Skill—Observation and Deduction
This chapter illustrates again the importance of careful observation and knowledge of cultural background. In 6:7, the Philistine diviners advise their rulers to use cows that have calved but have never been yoked and to take the calves away. Why? Cows do not usually leave their suckling calves, and cows that have not been trained to haul carts would be especially unwilling.

For Thought and Discussion: What kind of belief in the God of Israel does 1 Samuel 4:1-6:12 suggest the Philistines had? How is this like and unlike the way God wants us to believe in Him?

For Thought and Discussion: Both the Philistines and the Israelites thought the ark was a potent symbol of God's presence and a sort of lucky charm. To what extent were they right, and to what extent were they wrong?

Beth Shemesh (6:9,12-13). A town of Judah near the Philistine border.

5. What parallels do you see between the events involving the ark while it was among the Philistines and those that occurred when it was returned to Israel (6:19-7:1)?

_____

_____

_____

_____

_____

6. What did the Israelites of Beth Shemesh learn from their experience with the ark (6:20)?

_____

_____

For Thought and Discussion: Is there anything in the New Testament or the experience of the Church that is lethal in its effects if not treated with reverence? Explain. (Consider Acts 5:1-11, 1 Corinthians 11:27-30.)

Optional Application: God's presence among His people did not mean they were immune from His judgment (6:19-20). Does your relationship with God lead you to reverence Him properly? How can you give practical expression to such reverence?

7. From all that happened in relation to the ark, both in Philistia and in Israel, how would you describe what the ark represented?

Holy (6:20). The word means "separate" or "set apart." The ancients divided things and beings into two categories: the holy and the common (Leviticus 10:10). Holy things and beings were utterly different from, utterly alien to, common things and ordinary creatures. It was impossible for common things and unholy people to come into contact with holy ones, so the ancients had rites for hallowing things and people.

To the pagans, the gods and all that belonged to them were holy. However, the Lord labored throughout Israel's history to teach that only He and what belonged to Him were holy. Likewise, holiness implied primarily power and otherness to pagans, but the Lord insisted that holiness had a moral element. In Canaanite religion, cult prostitutes were called "holy women." But because moral purity was an essential trait of the Holy One of Israel, He declared it an essential trait of holiness and holy people.

Samuel at Mizpah (7:2-17)

Baals and Ashtoreths (7:4). Baal and Ashtoreth were the most important male and female Canaanite

52

gods. *Baal* literally meant "lord," "master," "owner," or "husband," but the term came to be applied to the deity who supposedly presided over thunder and rain, and so determined the fertility of the soil. Ashtoreth (also called Ashtaroth, Astarte, and Ishtar), was the goddess of war, love, and fertility. The worship of both gods included immoral practices, such as ritual sex and other magical rites to attain fertility. The Lord regarded them as heinous, and His prophets spared no effort to combat their worship. (See, for instance, the battle over rain and fire power in 1 Kings 17:1-18:46.)

The "Baals and Ashtoreths" were probably the stone pillars and wooden poles used to represent the deities in their shrines.

Mizpah (7:5). A town in Benjamin, about seven and a half miles north of Jerusalem.

Drew water and poured it out before the LORD (7:6). The Law never mentions this ceremony, so its meaning is uncertain. David did it as an offering to the Lord and as a symbol of the blood of men who had risked their lives to do him a kindness (2 Samuel 23:13-17). Here, the Israelites may have been expressing sorrow, humility, and repentance for their desperate condition (compare 1 Samuel 1:15, Psalm 62:8, Lamentations 2:19).

Leader (7:6). Traditionally, "judge." This was Israel's highest political office between the death of Joshua and the inauguration of the monarchy. The judge had judicial and military authority over whole tribes or even the entire nation, but unlike kingship the office was not hereditary. Rather, each judge was chosen and empowered by God. However, their divine appointment did not normally make them priests or give them the right to serve as spiritual leaders or as mediators between God and His people. Samuel exercised religious as well as judicial authority because his mother had consecrated him to God's service, he was probably of a priestly family, he grew up with Eli the priest, and he was gifted as a prophet as well as a judge.

For Further Study: Compare the call to return to the Lord "with all your hearts" (1 Samuel 7:3) to Deuteronomy 6:4-5; 11:1,13,22; 19:9; 30:6,16,20; Joshua 22:5; 23:11.

For Thought and Discussion: What does 1 Samuel 5:1-7:17 suggest about the extent to which God's honor depends on the obedience of His people?

For Thought and Discussion: Does the fact that the Lord sometimes miraculously intervenes on behalf of His people (7:7-10) mean that we should concentrate exclusively on "spiritual" rather than "worldly" preparations for an enterprise? Why or why not?

8. How did the Israelites show their determination to seek the Lord only (7:2-6)?

_____

_____

_____

_____

_____

9. What do you think would be the modern equivalents of these actions?

_____

_____

_____

_____

_____

10. How did God convince Israel to accept and appreciate Samuel's leadership (7:7-17)?

_____

_____

_____

_____

_____

11. Compare the Israelites' attitude toward themselves when threatened by the Philistines in chapter 7 to the attitude they showed in chapter 4 (4:3, 7:7-8). What similarities and differences do you observe?

_____

_____

_____

_____

_____

12. What do you think 7:10-11 was designed to teach Israel?

_____

_____

_____

_____

_____

_____

Optional Application: How do you think you should respond when threatened by enemies? Are there any examples to follow or avoid in 4:3 or 7:7-8?

Optional Application: Does God deserve the same awe and reverence He deserved in Samuel's day? If so, how can you take His holiness seriously in your actions?

Your response

> **Study Skill—Periodic Review and Outlining**
> When you come to the end of a major section of a book, it is a good time to pull together what you have studied in some way. An outline or chart of some kind is helpful. In this lesson, you will make a simple outline of chapters 1 through 7. In lesson sixteen, you will learn how to make a chart of the book.

13. Chapters 1 through 7 are the first major section of the book. Look back at what you wrote about this section in your overview (questions 1-3 on pages 16-17). Look also at the outlines in lesson one (page 19). Below, start an outline of 1 Samuel by giving titles to the major section and the secondary divisions. Try to show what each section contributes to the overall message of the book.

1:1-7:17 _____

_____

   1:1-3:21 _____

   _____

   4:1-7:17 _____

   _____

Optional Application: Examine your life to see whether your faith is compromised by reliance on "false gods"—anyone or anything other than the Lord. How can you turn to the Lord with all your heart? What practical steps, including but not limited to prayer, will this require?

For Further Study:
a. The books of Samuel stress the importance of the chosen leader in the lives of God's people. Is this emphasis consistent with the rest of Scripture?
b. What should be your attitude toward human leaders, both political and religious? What does the Bible say about this?

14. If 1 Samuel is about how Israel shifted from leadership by judges under God to leadership by kings under God, what is the purpose of 1:1–7:17?

_____

_____

_____

_____

_____

_____

15. What one insight from 5:1–7:17 would you like to take to heart this week?

_____

_____

_____

_____

16. How would you like this truth to affect your thoughts and actions, your priorities and habits?

_____

_____

_____

_____

_____

_____

17. What practical steps can you take this week to begin letting this happen, by God's grace?

_____

_____

_____

_____

_____

_____

18. List any questions you have about 5:1-7:17.

_____

_____

_____

_____

For the group

Warm-up. Ask group members to tell one way in which they have experienced God's holiness. If they have trouble answering this question, ask what holiness is. If the group still has trouble with the question, drop it until you have discussed what happened to the Philistines and the people of Beth Shemesh when they treated the Holy One disrespectfully, and what happened to the Israelites when they finally took His holiness seriously.

Questions. As you examine what God did in these chapters, invite group members to share how they feel about His strong actions. Are they scary? Encouraging? Incomprehensible? Motivating?

One big issue regarding application is the extent to which God is today as He was in Samuel's time. Does He afflict those who dishonor Him in such dramatic ways? Does He intervene in situations miraculously? Why or why not? What evidence can you cite? To what extent are His methods now like and unlike what they were then? To what extent is His character the same? To what extent are His expectations of His people constant? And finally, how are you going to act in light of the conclusions you have drawn?

Prayer. Thank God for displaying His holiness—His awesome power and purity—in Israel's history and your own lives. Ask Him to help you take His holiness seriously enough to turn to Him with all your hearts and put away your foreign gods. Ask Him to show each of you His holiness in unforgettable ways.

1. "Dagon," *The International Standard Bible Encyclopedia*, volume 1, edited by Geoffrey Bromiley (Grand Rapids, Michigan: William B. Eerdmans Publishing Company, 1979), page 851; *The NIV Study Bible*, page 382.

1 SAMUEL 8:1-10:27

"Give Us a King!"

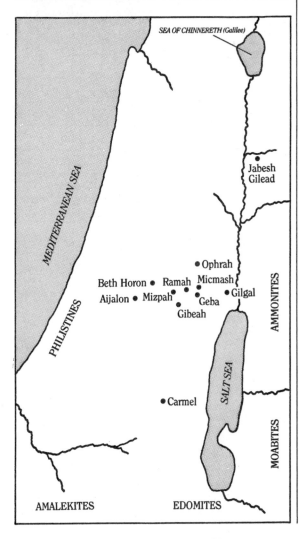

SEA OF CHINNERETH (Galilee)

MEDITERRANEAN SEA

Jabesh
Gilead

Ophrah
Beth Horon • Ramah Micmash
Aijalon • Mizpah • Geba • Gilgal
Gibeah

PHILISTINES

AMMONITES

SALT SEA

Carmel

MOABITES

AMALEKITES   EDOMITES

59

So far, 1 Samuel has focused on the miraculous birth, call, and ministry of Samuel, the prophet and judge of Israel. We've seen God in control in Israel's defeat and the loss of the ark, and God in control in the ark's return and Israel's victory. The years pass, and Samuel grows old as a good and godly judge.

These next three chapters are pivotal for the rest of Israel's history. What happens when the good judge approaches the end of his ministry? Read 8:1-10:27, preferably in two different translations.

1. Summarize in two or three sentences what happens in each of the following passages.

   8:1-22 _____

   _____

   _____

   _____

   9:1-10:8 _____

   _____

   _____

   _____

   10:9-27 _____

   _____

   _____

   _____

Israel seeks a king (8:1-22)

2. What reasons did the elders of Israel give for wanting a king (8:1-5)?

   _____

   _____

   _____

   _____

3. Why did they really want a king (8:20)?

_____

_____

_____

_____

_____

4. Why was their desire sinful (8:7-8, 10:19, 12:12)?

_____

_____

_____

_____

_____

5. What was wrong with being like the nations (1 Samuel 8:20)? See Deuteronomy 7:6-11.

_____

_____

_____

_____

_____

6. What did God command Samuel to do about the request for a king (8:7-9,21-22)?

_____

_____

_____

_____

_____

For Thought and Discussion: Do chapters 1-7 suggest that it was reasonable that the Israelites lost their trust in God's ability to lead and protect them? Why or why not?

For Thought and Discussion: Instead of demanding a king, what request could Israel have made that would have pleased the Lord?

Optional Application: Do you treat God as your King, or do you seek other sources of protection? How do your actions show this? How can you treat God as your King this week?

61

Optional Application: Consider what Samuel did when the people made a request that displeased him (8:6). What might he have done instead? How is 8:6 an example for you to follow?

For Further Study:
a. In Judges 8:22-23 and 9:1-57, read about another warning concerning the dangers of monarchy.
b. See how Samuel's predictions of the actions and effects of monarchy were fulfilled (1 Kings 12:1-15).

For Thought and Discussion: How can 1 Samuel 8 help us understand when desires that are legitimate in themselves may become harmful and wrong?

What the king . . . will do (8:11). "Using a description of the policies of contemporary Canaanite kings [8:11-17], Samuel warns the people of the burdens associated with the type of kingship they long for."[1]

Tenth (8:15). A tenth was the customary king's tax. The Lord demanded a tenth of each family's income as His royal portion (Leviticus 27:30-33, Numbers 18:26, Deuteronomy 14:22-29). Lands, crops, animals, and people belonged to the Lord as Israel's Great King.

7. In his response to Israel, what does Samuel try to explain (8:11-18)?

_____

_____

_____

_____

_____

8. How was Israel's king supposed to be different from the pagan kings (Deuteronomy 17:14-20)?

_____

_____

_____

_____

_____

_____

9. How successful was Samuel in getting his warning through to Israel (1 Samuel 8:19-22)?

_____

_____

_____

Samuel anoints Saul (9:1-10:8)

For Thought and Discussion: Do the prophets in 1 Samuel spend most of their time foretelling the future, declaring God's current will, or a mixture of both?

Prophet . . . seer (9:9). Along with the general term
"man of God," the word "seer" was another,
older way of referring to a prophet. The Hebrew
word is a participle of the verb "to see," but it
does not indicate that visions or dreams were
always the way God spoke to the prophet. Just
as in English, "see" was used metaphorically to
mean "perceive" or "understand."[2] God apparently revealed His will to Samuel verbally rather
than visually (3:2-14; 8:6-9,21-22; 9:15-17;
15:10-11; 16:1-2,6-12).

   The Hebrew word for "prophet" comes
from the verb "to call." First Samuel 3, Isaiah 6,
and Jeremiah 1 all illustrate why prophets were
named "called ones."

High place (9:12). It was a Canaanite custom to
build altars on hills. Thus when the Israelites
entered Canaan, they found pagan places of
worship and sacrifice scattered throughout the
land. At the time of 9:12, Israel's central sanctuary was not in use because the ark was sepa-
rated from the tabernacle. Shiloh had been de-
stroyed, and Eli's priestly family was decimated.
So, Samuel was apparently performing sacrifices
at local altars around the country. Samuel's
action presumably did not involve pagan practices, but later the Israelites continued to use
those high places for Canaanite-style worship
after the Temple was built in Jerusalem. The
use of sites long associated with Canaanite worship became a source of contamination for
Israel, so the prophets eventually condemned it
(1 Kings 3:2; 2 Kings 17:7-18, 21:2-9, 23:4-25).

Anoint (9:16). Consecrating a person as priest (Exodus 29:7), prophet (1 Kings 19:16), or king
(1 Samuel 10:1) involved pouring spiced olive
oil on his head. Oil seems to have symbolized
favor, blessing, and prosperity, and anointing
signified separation to the Lord for a particular
task and divine equipping for the task.[3]

   While prophets and priests were anointed,
the term "anointed one" was usually reserved
for kings (but see Zechariah 4:14). The Hebrew

For Further Study:
On Saul's desire to
give a gift to the
prophet, see 1 Kings
14:3; 22:6,8,18;
2 Kings 4:42;
5:15-16. How did pay-
ing prophets ulti-
mately affect their
performance?

term is *meshiach*, from which we get "Messiah"
and the Greek translation, "Christ."

Leg (9:24). This piece was normally reserved for
consecrated priests (Leviticus 7:32-33).

10. What impressions do you get of Saul's character
from 9:2-21?

_____

_____

_____

_____

_____

11. How would you evaluate Saul's concern to offer
a gift to the man of God (9:7)?

_____

_____

_____

_____

12. What signs of God's sovereignty and compassion
over the great and small affairs of life do you
find in 9:1–10:8?

_____

_____

_____

_____

_____

Saul made king (10:9-27)

Procession of prophets (10:5,10). "Small communities of men . . . banded together in spiritually

decadent times for mutual cultivation of their religious zeal."[4] They were called the "sons of the prophets" (1 Kings 20:35; 2 Kings 2:3-15; 4:1,38; 5:22; 6:1; 9:1). "Sons" meant members of a group, not necessarily biological offspring. The great prophets, like Samuel and Elijah were often mentors to the prophetic communities.

Is Saul also among the prophets? . . . *And who is their father?* (10:11-12). It may be that the observers knew enough about Saul to be astonished to find him among men passionately devoted to God. Or, the questions may be insults to prophets ("What was he [Saul], a respectable local citizen, doing in the presence of these roaming madmen of unknown and dubious antecedents?"[5]). The second question may be a gibe about Samuel, the prophets' spiritual father. Again, it may be a recognition that God is the Father of prophetic inspiration and can give it to anyone, even Saul.[6]

Benjamin was chosen (10:20). Probably by casting lots (14:41-42). The high priest wore an outer garment called an ephod (2:28; see the note on 14:3), in which he carried the Urim and Thummim. We don't know exactly what these were, but they seem to have been small stones or lots that were cast like dice to gain yes-or-no answers from the Lord (14:36-37,41-42; 22:10; 23:1-4,6,9-12). The assumption was that God would sovereignly control how they fell so as to reveal the correct answer (Proverbs 16:33).

Regulations of the kingship (10:25). Probably the laws relating to and limiting the authority of Israel's king (Deuteronomy 17:14-20). God may have revealed further guidelines through Samuel to show clearly how Israel's king must be different from pagan kings and how the monarchy would not conflict with the Lord's status as Great King.

For Thought and Discussion: Does God reveal and confirm His will today in the same ways that He did it in Samuel's day? How does He reveal and confirm His will today? What evidence can you cite?

13. Why do you think Samuel prophesied to Saul some specific events that were about to happen to him (10:2-10)?

For Thought and Discussion: What did the "troublemakers" expect of a king (10:27)? Was this a godly expectation? Why or why not?

For Thought and Discussion: To what extent do the first eight chapters of 1 Samuel reflect progress in Israel's history, and to what extent do they show repetition?

14. How was Saul divinely prepared as well as divinely chosen to lead the nation (10:6-7,9-12)?

_____

_____

_____

_____

15. How do we know that Saul's elevation to the throne was not the result of his personal ambition (9:1-10:27)?

_____

_____

_____

_____

16. Why were "the regulations of the kingship" (10:25) important?

_____

_____

_____

_____

Your response

17. What lesson from 8:1-10:27 seems most personally relevant to you?

_____

_____

66

_____

_____

_____

18. How would you like this to affect your life?

_____

_____

_____

_____

19. What can you do to act on this truth during the coming week?

_____

_____

_____

_____

20. List any questions you have about 8:1-10:27.

_____

_____

_____

For the group

Warm-up. Ask, "What are the advantages to God's people of a strong national leader? What are the disadvantages?" Start group members thinking about themselves and their nation, so that they can better identify with Israel in its situation: disunified, threatened by enemies, in spiritual disarray.

Questions. The important issues in this lesson are:

1. How have chapters 1 through 7 prepared the reader for the request for a king?

2. How should a king under the covenant differ from a pagan king?
3. What were Israel's motives for desiring a king, and what was wrong with them?
4. Saul's character—What evidence is there already that he is unlikely to be the kind of king God wants?

Prayer. Praise the Lord for being your King and for all that this entails. Thank Him for the leaders He has given you as His servants. Ask Him to show you how to treat Him as your King this week.

Two Views on Monarchy

Many scholars believe that the author of 1 and 2 Samuel incorporated two different opinions about the monarchy, one positive and one negative. According to them, some people in the author's time were in favor of monarchy, while others were hostile to it. In the books of Samuel, the prophet is the spokesman for the anti-monarchists, while other passages portray the monarchy as more fully God's will.

It is undeniable that the Lord sometimes rebukes the people for wanting a king, but at other times declares it to be His desire and blessing for them to have one. But the tension is not due to disagreements in the time of the author (although these may have existed). Instead, the tension is between the Lord's desire that Israel have a king for His right reasons and His disgust at the people's wrong reasons for wanting one. As the books of Samuel progress, we will find Saul embodying God's rebuke for Israel's wrong motives, and David exemplifying God's right reasons for establishing the kingship.

---

1. *The NIV Study Bible*, page 385.
2. G. V. Smith, "Prophet, Prophecy," *The International Standard Bible Encyclopedia*, volume 3, page 987.
3. *The NIV Study Bible*, page 387.
4. *The NIV Study Bible*, page 388.
5. D. F. Payne, "1 Samuel," *The New Bible Commentary: Revised*, edited by Donald Guthrie, et al. (Grand Rapids, Michigan: William B. Eerdmans Publishing Company, 1970), page 292.
6. *The NIV Study Bible*, page 388.

1 SAMUEL 11:1-12:25

Victory and Warning

When the Israelites begged for a king, the Lord rebuked their motives but agreed to grant their request. He told Samuel to anoint Saul privately, then designated His choice publicly through the ceremony of lots. Some Israelites, however, were unconvinced (10:27). Israel's leaders were traditionally revealed through great deeds inspired by the Spirit of God. Until they saw this, all Israel would not recognize Saul as king. So, Saul went home (10:26) to work on his father's land and wait for the Lord to take the next step. Read 11:1-12:25.

Saul rescues Jabesh (11:1-13)

1. What prompted Saul's first public action (11:1-6)?

_____

_____

_____

_____

_____

Ammonite (11:1). They were descended from Lot, Abraham's nephew, by an incestuous union

For Further Study:
Use a concordance to
trace the relationship
and conflicts between
Israel and the
Ammonites.

(Genesis 19:31-38). They were thus distantly related to Israel, but not loved. The territory they occupied was northeast of the Dead Sea, across the Jordan River from Israel (see page 59). Seeing Israel hard pressed by the Philistines on the west, the Ammonites seized the chance to move against Israel on the east.

Make a treaty with us (11:1). The inhabitants of Jabesh Gilead tried to buy Nahash off. The term translated "treaty" is rendered elsewhere as "covenant," especially when used of Israel's relationship to God. The problem with their stratagem is not just that Nahash rejected it, but that God had forbidden Israel to make any treaties with the people of Canaan (Exodus 34:12-16, Deuteronomy 7:2). The Jabeshites would have been willing to serve, but God was working for their salvation.

Gouge out (11:2). "Besides causing humiliation . . . the loss of the right eye would destroy the military capability of the archers."[1]

Messengers throughout Israel (11:3). Nahash apparently felt so convinced of his military superiority, even over all Israel, that he consented to this unusual request. Israel's leader, Samuel, was elderly, and the tribes were not tightly unified but only a loose confederacy at this time. The messengers from Jabesh Gilead had to contact the elders of the various tribes individually; they could not simply appeal to some central authority (such as a king or a permanent executive body) that could command the whole nation's obedience. In fact, it was just this lack of a strong central authority that had caused the people to demand a king in the first place (8:5,20).

2. Summarize the chain of events that led to the rescue of Jabesh Gilead (11:3-11).

_____

_____

_____

3. What was Saul's role in all of this?

_____

_____

_____

_____

For Thought and Discussion: Since Nahash rejected the Jabeshites' offer of submission, what seems to have been his objective in attacking this city (11:1-2)?

4. Why did this event convince all Israel that Saul was the Lord's choice to be king (11:6-12)?

_____

_____

_____

_____

_____

The Spirit of God came upon him in power (11:6).
This phrase occurs often (Numbers 24:2;
Judges 3:10; 6:34; 11:29; 13:25; 14:6,19; 15:14;
1 Samuel 16:13; 1 Chronicles 12:18; 2 Chronicles 15:1; 20:14; 24:20). It normally speaks of a
special empowerment granted to someone by
God to accomplish a particular task. It is never
used of a conversion experience in the New Testament sense. Nor does it imply that everything
the individual does is according to God's will
(Judges 11:29-31 is an example). Israel's judges
were usually marked out in this way.

5. What does 11:1-15 suggest about Saul's moral
and spiritual character at this time?

_____

71

For Further Study:
Gilgal was significant in Israel's history. See Joshua 4:19; 5:1-10; 9:6; 10:6,43; 14:6; Judges 2:1.

For Thought and Discussion: Since the kingship was hereditary while the judgeship was not, do you think the transition from judges to kings encouraged or discouraged dependence upon the Lord? Why?

The kingship confirmed (11:14-12:25)

6. Summarize the main points in each part of Samuel's farewell address to the nation.

12:1-5 _____

_____

_____

_____

12:6-13 _____

_____

_____

_____

12:14-18 _____

_____

_____

_____

12:19-25 _____

_____

_____

_____

7. How would you express the gist of his message as a whole?

_____

_____

_____

_____

_____

Optional Application: Chapters 11-12 show us two men committed to serving God's people. In what one specific way can you serve others in the Body of Christ this week with the same commitment? What might it cost you to do this, and are you willing to pay the cost?

Testify against me (12:3). As he passes the leadership to Saul, Samuel demands that Israel compare his performance to the moral guidelines laid down by God's Law.

_____

8. Why do you think Samuel emphasized his own record in 12:3-5? What point was he making?

_____

_____

_____

_____

_____

Optional Application: Samuel's life was a model of integrity (12:3-5). Could you stand up and say what Samuel said? Reflect on your own moral standards and performance. Are there any habits or choices you need to change?

Thunder and rain (12:17-18). In Palestine the rainy season is October/November to March/April. The wheat harvest takes place in June, a time when rain is rare. Samuel's ability to call upon the Lord to send rain was a miracle that validated his words. Also, it demonstrated that the Lord, not Baal, was the true ruler of the rains and alone merited Israel's worship and trust.

9. On this occasion when Saul was confirmed as king, how was the Lord's supreme Kingship also reaffirmed?

11:13 _____

_____

11:15 _____

_____

73

For Thought and Discussion: a. What would continue to be the prophet's role in Israel (12:23)?

b. Are these activities important today? Explain.

For Thought and Discussion: Why would it be a sin for Samuel to cease to pray for Israel (12:23)?

Optional Application: Would it be a sin for you to cease to pray for someone?

12:7-15 _____

_____

_____

12:16-18 _____

_____

_____

12:20-25 _____

_____

_____

10. In the transition to monarchy, what had changed, and what had not (12:12-25)?

changed _____

_____

_____

_____

_____

not changed _____

_____

_____

_____

_____

11. Observe the words Samuel used to describe how Israel should treat the Lord: "fear . . . serve . . . obey . . . do not rebel . . . follow" (12:14; compare 12:24). How would you describe in your own words the actions and attitudes Samuel was urging?

_____

_____

_____

_____

_____

12. What emphases in 12:1-25 are still relevant to Christians today?

_____

_____

_____

_____

_____

_____

_____

Your response

Optional Application: How can you fear, serve, obey, and follow the Lord this week?

For Thought and Discussion: According to 12:1-25, why would it be a false security to trust in a king without obeying the Lord?

For Further Study: Compare Samuel's farewell address to the Apostle Paul's final words to the Ephesian elders (Acts 20:17-35). What similarities do you see?

Study Skill—Application
At the end of each lesson of this study is a series of questions to help you plan an application step by step. Observe the progression of the following questions. Use it as a model when you study the Bible on your own.

13. What one truth from 11:1-12:25 would you like to take to heart and apply this week?

_____

_____

_____

_____

14. How have you already seen this truth active in your life?

_____

_____

_____

_____

_____

15. How do you fall short or want to grow in this
area? How would you like this truth to affect
your thoughts, actions, habits, and priorities?

_____

_____

_____

_____

_____

16. What practical steps can you take to cooperate
with God in letting this happen?

_____

_____

_____

_____

_____

17. How can you make sure you remember to do
this? (Tape a note on your refrigerator, in your
car, or in your office. Ask a friend to remind
you.)

_____

_____

_____

18. List any questions you have about 11:1-12:25.

_____

_____

_____

_____

For the group

Warm-up. Ask each person to think of a Christian leader to whom he or she is in submission. Ask everyone not to name names. Then say, "What evidence is there that the Spirit of God is active through that person?" In 11:1-12:25, we see the Spirit behind Saul's military prowess, Samuel's moral integrity, Samuel's ability to call upon the Lord for miracles, Samuel's intercession for the people, and his ability to teach them what is right. At some point in your discussion, ask the group to compare these evidences of the Spirit to the evidences they see in the lives of their leaders.

Questions. Focus on what changed and what remained the same when Israel shifted from judges to kings. How was the prophet's role affected? How was the Lord's place in people's lives supposed to change or not change? How were the terms of the covenant affected, and the moral demands on Israel's leaders and people?

To some extent, the transition from judges to kings was a unique event in Israel's history. We need to be careful in applying what is said to Israel on this occasion to ourselves. For example, are Christian leaders expected to be great warriors because that was how the Lord validated Saul? If so, in what sense, and why? If not, why not? Again, what about the moral demands the Lord placed on the people? Do they apply to us? Try to come up with some ways these chapters are relevant to you, and some action you plan to take in response.

Prayer. Thank God for raising up leaders for defense, for teaching, for prayer, and for moral example. Ask Him to make you the kind of people He desires—who fear, serve, obey, and follow Him. Ask Him to make your leaders more and more the kind He desires. Praise Him as your King.

Samuel, the Covenant Mediator

Samuel was in many ways a second Moses. Observe what the two men had in common:

1. Providential infancy (Exodus 2:1-10, 1 Samuel 1:9-20).

(continued on page 78)

(continued from page 77)

2. Son of godly parents (1 Samuel 1:1-28, Hebrews 11:23).

3. Raised in a house destined for judgment (Exodus 2:10, 1 Samuel 2:11-26).

4. Called by God (Exodus 3:1-4:17, 1 Samuel 3:4-14).

5. Used by God to liberate Israel from foreign oppressor (Exodus 3:10, 12:29-14:31; 1 Samuel 7:5-14).

6. Interceded for Israel (Exodus 5:22, 32:11-14; 1 Samuel 7:5-9).

7. Built an altar (Exodus 24:4, 1 Samuel 7:17).

8. Offered sacrifices on the nation's behalf (Exodus 24:4-8, 1 Samuel 7:9-10).

9. Led the people in sanctification (Exodus 19:10-15, 1 Samuel 7:3-4).

10. Led the nation in battle as an intercessor, not a warrior (Exodus 17:8-13; 1 Samuel 7:5-14, 11:7-15).

11. Erected a monument (Exodus 24:4, 1 Samuel 7:12).

12. Adjudicated civil disputes (Exodus 18:13-26, 1 Samuel 7:15-17).

13. Demonstrated God's power in miracles (Exodus 9:22-26, 1 Samuel 12:16-18).

14. Mediated God's word (Deuteronomy 5, 1 Samuel 3:21-4:1).

15. Recorded God's word in a book (Exodus 24:3-4, 1 Samuel 10:25).

16. Inaugurated a new phase in the nation's history (Exodus 19:1-6, 1 Samuel 8:4-9).

17. Consecrated the new leader of God's choice (Numbers 27:15-23, 1 Samuel 9:27-10:1).

18. Concluded his ministry by exorting Israel to be faithful to the Lord (Deuteronomy, 1 Samuel 12).

Like Moses, Samuel was Israel's covenant mediator, the man who stood between Israel and the Lord to speak the Lord's word to Israel and to intercede for the nation before its King (Deuteronomy 18:15-19). In order to understand what happens in 1 Samuel 13:1-15:35, it is crucial to grasp Samuel's status as covenant mediator.

1. *The NIV Study Bible*, page 389.

1 SAMUEL 13:1-14:52

First Disobedience

Saul is now king, and Samuel has given up his political responsibilities. But the prophet is still Israel's spiritual leader. As mediator between God and the nation, he is responsible to direct Saul in the will of God. For Saul's kingship is not absolute; he is only the vice-regent of the Great King and is answerable to His Law and instructions. The test of Saul's fitness to rule will be: Will he obey God's word through the Law and the prophet?

In recounting the results of this test, chapters 13 through 15 are a unit. But in order to avoid too lengthy a lesson, we have divided them between lessons seven and eight. However, begin now by reading all of 13:1-15:35, noting how the episodes fit together to make their point.

1. Using the map on page 59, sort out in your mind the stages of the conflict described in 13:1-15:35. Write down a summary of what happens at each stage.

   a. Saul's army at Micmash, Jonathan's at Gibeah, the Philistines at Geba (13:1-4)

   _____

   _____

   _____

   b. Saul's army at Gilgal, the Philistines at Micmash (13:5-14)

_____

_____

_____

c. Saul's army at Gibeah, the Philistines at
Micmash (13:15-22)

_____

_____

_____

d. Saul's army at Gibeah, the Philistines at
Micmash pass (13:23–14:19)

_____

_____

_____

e. Saul pursues the Philistines from Micmash
past Beth Aven to Aijalon (14:20-46)

_____

_____

_____

f. Saul attacks Amalek (15:1-11)

_____

_____

_____

g. Saul moves to Carmel, then Gilgal; Samuel
goes to Gilgal (15:12-33)

_____

_____

_____

h. Samuel to Ramah, Saul to Gibeah (15:34-35)

_____

_____

_____

The first test (13:1-15)

_____

He reigned over Israel forty-two years (13:1). The
Hebrew text of 1 Samuel suffered in transmis-
sion, and the length of Saul's reign is not clear.
Paul implied that it lasted forty years (Acts
13:21).
    If Saul was thirty in 11:1–12:25, then
quite a few years have passed between chapters
12 and 13. Saul's oldest son has had time to
grow up and become a commander of one of
Saul's armies.

_____

2. How would you describe the Israelites' emo-
tional state when the Philistines came against
them (13:5-8)?

_____

_____

_____

3. According to Saul, what prompted him to offer
the sacrifice, rather than waiting for Samuel as
instructed (13:11-12)?

_____

_____

_____

_____

4. How did Samuel react to Saul's unauthorized
action (13:13-14)?

_____

_____

**For Thought and
Discussion:** What do
you learn about the
balance of power
between Israel and
Philistia from 13:5-7?

**Optional
Application:** Do you
ever disobey the Lord
when you are afraid
He doesn't know what
He's doing and isn't
taking care of you?
How should you act in
light of 13:1-15?

81

For Thought and Discussion: Does the relationship between king and prophet in Israel have any parallels in the Body of Christ today? Explain. How are things similar and different now?

_____

_____

Foolishly (13:13). In Hebrew, a fool was someone morally as well as intellectually lacking (compare 1 Samuel 25:25, 26:21; 2 Samuel 24:10).

5. Why was it so important that the king obey what the prophet said the Lord had commanded (Deuteronomy 12:13-14, 17:18-20, 18:15-19)?

_____

_____

_____

_____

_____

_____

6. What are the positive and negative aspects of the prophecy Samuel gave to Saul (13:13-14)?

positive _____

_____

_____

_____

negative _____

_____

_____

_____

A man after his own heart (13:14). This is the first indication that Saul was unqualified at the deepest level for his position. Though he had

82

been divinely appointed and confirmed by the people, he was not above replacement (compare 2:30). While Saul's heart had been changed by God (10:9), he did not necessarily experience conversion in the New Testament sense nor a complete spiritual transformation.

Jonathan's boldness (13:16-14:52)

7. After Samuel left Saul, only six hundred of the original Israelite troops stayed with the king (13:15). Besides an overwhelming numerical superiority, what other advantage did the Philistines possess (13:16-22)?

_____

_____

_____

_____

_____

Raiding parties (13:17). "The purpose of these Philistine contingents was not to engage the Israelites in battle, but to plunder the land and demoralize its inhabitants."[1]

Not . . . a sword or spear (13:22). Without blacksmiths to work iron, the Israelites were left to fight with slingshots and bows and arrows.

8. What role did Saul's son Jonathan play in the next stage of the conflict (13:23-14:23)?

_____

_____

_____

_____

_____

For Further Study: The many times the word *heart* appears in the Old Testament should convince us that Israel's devotion to the Lord was not to be a matter of ritual only. Use a concordance to find references to *heart,* beginning with Exodus 25:2; Deuteronomy 4:29; 5:29; 6:5-6; 8:5; 10:12,16; 11:13,18; Joshua 22:5; 24:23; 1 Samuel 2:1; 7:3. How would you describe in your own words the relationship God wanted with His people?

For Thought and Discussion: What do the references to Jonathan in 14:1-52 imply about his character and faith?

83

For Thought and Discussion: a. What attitude toward the war did Saul show by making everyone fast until "*I* have avenged *myself* on *my* enemies" (14:24)?

b. What was wrong with this attitude?

Optional Application: Have you ever turned a mission from the Lord into a personal crusade that overran others' needs and common sense? Pray about this, and ask the Lord to help you keep your own pride from interfering with His missions.

Wearing an ephod (14:3). The term was used of two or three different things. The ephod worn by the high priest was a "sleeveless garment . . . to which two shoulder pieces were attached and around which fitted a belt. To the shoulder pieces were affixed two onyx stones engraved with the names of the twelve tribes. . . . At the front of the garment . . . hung the breastpiece of twelve precious stones symbolizing the twelve tribes. . . ."[2]

Another kind of ephod was worn by priests, Samuel, David, and perhaps others (1 Samuel 2:18, 22:18; 2 Samuel 6:14). Some scholars think it was a kind of loincloth.[3] Others think it was "a close-fitting, sleeveless pullover, usually of hip length" worn over one's robe or tunic.[4]

9. How did God enable Israel to gain the upper hand against Philistia on this occasion (14:15,20)?

_____

_____

_____

_____

10. As the battle developed, what did Saul order the people not to do, and why (14:24)?

_____

_____

_____

_____

_____

11. What were three consequences of this order?

14:28-30 _____

_____

14:31-33 _____

_____

14:36-46 _____

_____

Saul built an altar (14:35). The Israelite troops were so hungry that they were slaughtering the Philistines' livestock and eating it without making sure that the blood had been drained. This violated the law that all animals killed for food be drained of blood, since it was forbidden to eat blood (Leviticus 17:10-14, 19:26; Deuteronomy 12:16). To prevent this breach of the Law, Saul hastily erected an altar to insure that all the animals were properly butchered.

---

12. What do Saul's order and its consequences say about his wisdom as a leader?

_____

_____

_____

_____

13. What indications are there that God had not yet abandoned Saul at this time (14:20-23,47-48)?

_____

_____

_____

_____

_____

Your response

14. What spiritual lessons, both positive and nega-

For Thought and Discussion: Remember that subtle observations lead to implicit clues in a narrative. What can you learn about Saul from the facts that . . .
  a. he had never heard of the great prophet Samuel (9:5-7)?
  b. people were surprised to find him among the prophets (10:11)?
  c. he had never before built an altar in all his years as king (14:35)?

For Thought and Discussion: What reasons did the troops give to keep Saul from afflicting Jonathan with the consequences of his rash curse (14:45)? Do you think this was valid? Why or why not?

85

tive, do you think the Holy Spirit intends us to learn through 13:1-14:52?

_____

_____

_____

_____

_____

_____

_____

15. What one of these lessons, or another insight from 13:1-14:52, would you like to put into practice in your current circumstances?

_____

_____

_____

_____

_____

16. What implications does this truth have for your life? How would you like it to affect what you think and do?

_____

_____

_____

_____

_____

17. What steps can you take to begin this process?

_____

_____

_____

_____

_____

_____

18. List any questions you have about 13:1-14:52.

_____

_____

_____

_____

For the group

Warm-up. Ask everyone to think of a time when he or she has done something foolish because of fear, because of a difficulty in fully trusting God. Let one or two people share their memories aloud, if they are willing to describe their inglorious moments. Remembering their own mistakes should help group members identify with Saul.

Read aloud and summarize. Have someone (or several people) read 13:1-14:52 aloud. Then go around the room, letting each person answer one of the parts of question 1 to summarize this whole section. Keeping chapter 15 in mind as you discuss 13 and 14 will make the themes of the section clearer. When you've gone through all of question 1, ask someone to summarize what chapters 13 through 15 are basically about.

Questions. Question 5 is crucial. God divided authority in Israel so that no one man could claim supremacy. Samuel was God's prophet, priest, and covenant mediator as Saul was God's king. Each had to submit to the other out of submission to the Lord (compare Ephesians 5:21). The king could not be above God's eternal written Word (the Law) nor His immediate spoken word (the prophet). Is any of this relevant today?

The marginal and numbered questions offer several issues you can explore and apply in these chapters. Choose one or two to delve into.

Prayer. Thank God for forgiving the times you have let fear or arrogance move you to fail Him and act foolishly. Ask Him to help you overcome both fear and pride, and to equip you to serve Him as men and women after His heart. Praise Him that He is worthy of your total trust, loyalty, and submission.

1. *The NIV Study Bible*, page 393.
2. "Ephod," *The Eerdmans Bible Dictionary*, edited by Allen C. Meyers (Grand Rapids, Michigan: William B. Eerdmans Publishing Company, 1987), page 342.
3. C. de Wit, "Dress," *The New Bible Dictionary*, second edition, edited by J.D. Douglas (Leicester, England: Inter-Varsity Press, 1982), page 291.
4. *The NIV Study Bible*, page 378.

1 SAMUEL 15:1-35

Second Disobedience

To test whether Saul truly trusted and submitted to his Lord, the Lord sent him to Gilgal to await Samuel for a week in the midst of a critical battle. Saul failed that test. Then he displayed his arrogance with a rash curse that nearly cost his son's life. But let no one say that the Lord is harsh or arbitrary. Saul will not be condemned on the basis of one mistake, but only if he shows persistent unrepentant sin. In 15:1-35 he gets his second chance to prove himself.

Read 15:1-35 again, keeping 13:1-14:52 in mind.

The second test (15:1-35)

"In [chapter 13] obedience was the stone on which Saul stumbled; here it is the rock that crushes him."[1]

Amalekites . . . Kenites (15:3,5). The Amalekites were descended from Esau (Genesis 36:12-16) and occupied the territory south of Israel known as the Negev. Though related to Israel, they appear in the Old Testament only as enemies of God. They were the first to attack the Hebrews after their liberation from Egypt (Exodus 17:8-13). Later, after Israel's refusal to enter the promised land, the Amalekites defeated them

89

For Further Study:
Compare 1 Samuel
15 to Joshua 7.

For Further Study:
In the book of Esther,
read how one of
Saul's descendants
received a chance to
make amends for
Saul's failure to kill
Agag, the Amalekite
king (Esther 2:5, 3:1).

(Numbers 14:41-45), and during the period of the judges they repeatedly harassed them (Judges 3:13, 6:3-40).

The Kenites, on the other hand, were a clan unrelated to Israel but had a generally good relationship with Israel from the exodus onward (Numbers 10:29, Judges 1:16). That is why Saul sought to spare them when he went against the Amalekites.

1. In the battle against Amalek, how closely did Saul's actions conform to the command he had received through Samuel (15:1-3,7-9,15,20-21)?

_____

_____

_____

_____

_____

Totally destroy (15:3). God had commanded Israel to utterly destroy the Canaanite tribes because their sinful religious practices threatened to corrupt His people (Deuteronomy 7:1-5,17-26). This destruction involved all of the people belonging to the group in question but not always all of their possessions (Joshua 6:17-21, 8:1-2). The divine command to destroy the Amalekites seems to have been motivated less by a concern for Israel's purity than by a decision to judge them for what they had done to Israel previously. God may also have been testing Saul's obedience again.

2. What did God say to Samuel about Saul's performance (15:10-11)?

_____

_____

_____

90

_____

_____

Grieved (15:11,35). The Bible sometimes speaks of
God repenting of (KJV) or regretting (NASB) a
certain action. Such a way of speaking is known
technically as an *anthropopathism*—ascribing
human emotions to God. (This is similar to
anthropomorphism—referring to God's "eyes,"
"hands," etc.) While such expressions are pow-
erful and moving, properly understanding them
is not always easy. It is crucial to first note what
they do *not* mean. That God repented does not
call into question either His omniscience or His
omnipotence by implying that He did not fore-
see what happened and/or was helpless to do
anything about it. Nor does it suggest that God
realized He had made a mistake.

What it does imply is, first, that God was
by no means emotionally indifferent to whether
or not people carried out His will. Second, it
indicates God's determination to take appropriate steps to remedy the situation. Finally, in
1 Samuel 15 we find that while there is a sense
in which God repented (15:11), there is a much
more fundamental sense in which He did not,
and cannot, repent, "for he is not a man, that
he should change his mind" (15:29).

3. What does 15:12-13 suggest about Saul's opinion of himself?

_____

_____

_____

4. Do you think Saul's justification for sparing the
best of the livestock was legitimate (15:15)?
Why or why not? (See 15:20-21,24.)

_____

_____

For Further Study:
Research other pas-
sages that use the
Hebrew term found in
15:11,29,35 to speak
of God's repentance,
grief, or relenting
(Genesis 6:5-7;
Exodus 32:12-14;
Numbers 23:19;
Deuteronomy 32:36;
Judges 2:18;
2 Samuel 24:16;
Psalm 90:13, 106:45,
110:4, 135:14).

**For Thought and
Discussion:** How are
the events of chapter
15 like and unlike
those of chapter 13?

**For Thought and
Discussion:** Is it
possible to obey the
spirit of a law without
obeying the letter of
it? Consider 15:1-29
and your own
experience.

91

Optional Application: What clear and direct orders has the Lord given you? Are you obeying Him completely or only partially?

Optional Application: Fear twice moved Saul to disobey God (13:11-12, 15:24). Has fear led you to disobey recently? Is it tempting you to do so now? If so, how can you overcome this temptation?

Optional Application: Pride also contributed to Saul's disobedience. Is pride a problem in any area of your life? Ask God to help you learn true selfless humility.

5. Summarize in a sentence or two the declaration of Samuel in 15:22-23.

6. How did this declaration affect Saul? (Compare 15:20-21 to 15:24-25.)

7. How does the judgment pronounced by Samuel in this situation differ from what he said in 13:13-14 (15:23,28)?

Your response

8. What spiritual lessons do you see illustrated in 15:1-35? (What do you learn about God's nature, His expectations of His people, how He deals with people?)

_____

_____

_____

_____

_____

_____

_____

_____

_____

9. Which one of the lessons you just wrote, or another insight from 15:1-35, would you like to take to heart this week?

_____

_____

_____

_____

_____

10. How do you fall short or need to grow in this area? How would you like it to affect you in a deeper way?

_____

_____

_____

_____

_____

11. What can you do this week to act on this desire?

_____

_____

For Thought and Discussion: How does Samuel model courage, compassion, and sternness in his response to the king in 13:13-15 and 15:13-35?

For Thought and Discussion: What similarities and differences do you see between the judgment upon Saul and that upon Eli at the beginning of the book? What might be the point of these parallels?

Optional Application: Are you more concerned with religious activities than with matters of basic righteousness and obedience (15:22)? Have you treated church attendance, Bible study, or other activities as substitutes for real intimacy with and obedience to God? Pray about this, and take action if necessary.

For Thought and Discussion: What does 15:22-35 imply about Samuel's personality and the depth of his relationship with the Lord?

_____

_____

_____

_____

12. In question 12 of lesson four, you outlined the
first major section of 1 Samuel. Below, continue
that outline by giving titles to each of the episodes of chapters 8 through 15. Use your
answers to questions 1 through 3 of lesson one
and the outlines there (pages 16-17, 19) for
help. Let your titles express the central point of
each episode, and how it relates to the overall
message of the book.

8:1-12:25 _____

_____

_____

    8:1-22 _____

    _____

    _____

    9:1-10:16 _____

    _____

    _____

    10:17-27 _____

    _____

    _____

    11:1-11 _____

    _____

    _____

    11:12-12:25 _____

    _____

    _____

13:1-15:35 _____

_____

_____

13:1-15 _____

_____

_____

13:16-14:52 _____

_____

_____

15:1-35 _____

_____

_____

13. List any questions you have about 15:1-35, or anything else in this lesson.

_____

_____

_____

_____

For the group

Warm-up. Ask, "What clear command has God given you that you should be obeying this week?" If no one can think of any commands, point out that the Bible is full of them. By the end of your meeting, make it a goal to help everyone face up to one thing the Lord desires of him or her. Connect this goal to the theme of 13:1-15:35—Saul's willful disobedience to known commands and the consequences of this.

Questions. It may seem astonishing that Saul's big sin was sparing an enemy's life and not wastefully butchering prime cattle. Ask the group how they feel about this. Does it make the Lord seem irrational and arbitrary? When you've let people express their feelings, explore why the Lord insisted on total destruction and what Saul's real reasons for disobedience were. Are we free to disobey the Lord when it seems more rational or humane to do so? Do any of you tend to evaluate the merits of God's commands before following them? What is good or bad about doing this? Are you comfortable submitting to a God who makes demands you find irrational or distasteful? These are some questions you might delve into.

Alternatively, you can discuss the quality of your obedience versus the quantity of your religious activity (consider Saul putting sacrifice before simple obedience), or how much you let fear or pride influence your actions.

Prayer. Thank the Lord for your leaders. To the extent that they are disobedient and willful like Saul, ask the Lord to train them and to teach you how to forgive. Ask the Lord to encourage and strengthen them, and to make them ever more disciplined and intimate with Him, as Samuel was. Then, pray for the same discipline and obedience for yourselves. Ask for the courage to overcome fear and pride.

1. Robert P. Gordon, *1 and 2 Samuel* (Exeter, England: The Paternoster Press, 1986), page 142.

1 SAMUEL 16:1-17:58

A Man After God's Heart

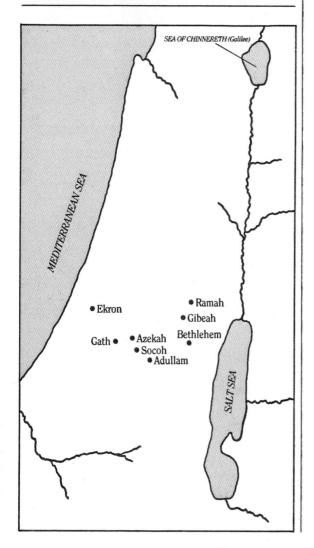

SEA OF CHINNERETH (Galilee)

MEDITERRANEAN SEA

• Ekron

• Ramah

• Gibeah

Gath •   • Azekah   Bethlehem
          • Socoh   •
            • Adullam

SALT SEA

For Further Study:
While the judges were raised up spontaneously by God, the kings were called or confirmed by prophets. Observe this in 1 Samuel 10:1; 1 Kings 1:32-39, 11:29-39, 19:15-16; 2 Kings 9:1-10.

For Further Study:
The ancients felt strongly about the superiority and priority of the firstborn, but the book of Genesis repeatedly stresses God's choice of a younger brother for special blessing or service (Genesis 17:18-21; 25:23; 27:27-29,39-40; 37:5-11). Why? (See Romans 9:16-21.)

No sooner had Saul been elevated to the throne than he disobeyed specific commands given through Samuel. As a result, the prophet predicted the end of Saul's rule and intimated that the Lord would raise up someone else to lead His people. In 16:1–17:58, we learn who that person was and what God saw in him. Read these chapters.

Samuel anoints David (16:1-13)

1. Samuel's mission in 16:1-13 is to anoint a new king. How is he supposed to present his errand to the public, and why (16:2-3)?

2. Why do you think Samuel assumes that Eliab is God's choice (16:6-7; compare 9:2, 10:23-24)?

3. How would you put into your own words what God says to Samuel in 16:7?

I have rejected him (16:1,7). The election and rejection spoken of in these chapters concerns not salvation but service. God had determined that David rather than anyone else would lead His people as their next king. Saul's rejection should not be interpreted as meaning that he "lost his salvation" in a New Testament sense. It simply shows that he was no longer qualified to be king because of his repeated disobedience. Similarly, David's brothers were rejected only in that they were not chosen to be king.

4. How important did David seem to his own family (16:11)?

_____

_____

_____

_____

_____

5. What happened when Samuel anointed David (16:13)? Explain in your own words.

_____

_____

_____

Tending the sheep (16:11). David is introduced as a shepherd, an Israelite metaphor for a ruler. In the Psalms, the prophetic books, and the New Testament, God's people are often described as a flock. God and the leaders who are supposed to represent Him are called shepherds (2 Samuel 5:2, 7:7-8; Psalm 23:1, 78:71-72; Ezekiel 34:1-31; John 10:1-18). From the Latin word for "shepherd," we get the English word *pastor*.

Compare the way Saul was introduced: vainly chasing wayward donkeys (1 Samuel 9:3; see Isaiah 1:3).

Optional Application: If you are in a position of choosing someone for leadership or partnership, ask the Lord to help you to choose someone with the heart He wants, and not to be distracted by outward appearances.

For Thought and Discussion: How did David's family illustrate 16:7?

For Further Study: Does the New Testament teach that the principle of election for special ministry is applicable today (Matthew 4:18-22; Luke 9:1-5, 10:1-12; Acts 9:1-6, 13:1-3; 1 Corinthians 12:27-31; 1 Timothy 3:1-13)? If so, how is it relevant? If not, why not?

For Thought and Discussion: Does 16:1-13 indicate why God chose David? If so, what reasons does it suggest? If not, why do you think it doesn't?

For Thought and
Discussion: a. In the
case of Saul's evil
spirit, how did the
Lord bring ultimate
good out of this
affliction?
    b. In what sense
are the evils you ex-
perience sent by the
Lord, and in what
sense is He not
responsible for your
afflictions?

For Further Study:
Read how another
spirit from God acts in
a negative way to
achieve God's ends in
1 Kings 22:19-23.

David the musician (16:14-23)

6. As he grew older, Saul began to experience fits
of depression, jealousy, and violence (19:9-10).
What caused his psychological problems?

15:24-26 _____

_____

_____

16:14 _____

_____

Study Skill—Hebrew Thought

Europeans and Americans are raised with a
system of thought that originated in ancient
Greece. This system stresses logic—the kind
mathematicians use to deduce axioms in
geometry, and the kind Sherlock Holmes
made famous for solving crimes. Greek logic
insists that opposites contradict each other
and cannot both be true.

By contrast, Hebrews believed that opposites are often both true. In the Bible we find
Jesus, the apostles, and the prophets often
holding apparently conflicting ideas in tension. In 1 Samuel 16:14, Saul's troubles are
attributed to "an evil spirit from the LORD." If
we look further, we find that in the Old Testament everything, including evil, is com-
monly traced back to God (Job 2:10, Isaiah
45:7, Amos 3:6), who is in some sense
responsible for it or the cause of it. At the
same time, the Scriptures affirm the absolute
holiness of God and never imply that evil has
its ultimate origin in Him. James 1:13-17
insists that God is not the source of temptations to do evil, but this "evil spirit from the
LORD" clearly moves Saul to attempt murder.

There is some merit in trying to logically
work out in what sense God is responsible for
evil such as Saul's "evil spirit," and in what
sense He is not. But it is more fruitful to ask
God for the Hebrew ability to hold apparent

(continued on page 101)

100

(continued from page 100)
contradictions in tension. We need a certain humility about our reasoning abilities. The Bible emphasizes God's absolute sovereignty and teaches that He is able to use even evil to achieve His own purposes, which are always good. How God can use evil for good is something we need to see in specific circumstances with the eyes of faith, not try to reduce to a series of logical axioms.

A further note on 1 Samuel 16:14: It was not unjust for God to afflict Saul; He was simply following the terms of His covenant with Israel. That covenant promised blessings, such as God's Spirit to equip Saul to be king (10:10, 11:6), if Saul was obedient. It promised curses, such as the Holy Spirit's departure and an evil spirit's torment, for disobedience.

For Thought and Discussion: a. Does God's judgment upon Saul seem unduly harsh? Why or why not? Compare the judgment upon Moses (Numbers 20:10-12).

b. What does this tell you about God's character and values?

c. Are Christians subject to any judgment in this life for disobedience? In what ways, or why not?

For Thought and Discussion: Why is it ironic that Saul became dependent upon David for his mental health (15:24-26, 16:13)?

7. Saul's servants suggested a musician like David as a remedy for his affliction (16:14-18). What was it about David that impressed his contemporaries (16:18)?

_____

_____

_____

_____

_____

8. Why do you think David's music was successful in overcoming the evil spirit upon Saul (16:13,23)?

_____

_____

_____

_____

_____

_____

For Thought and Discussion: How has the Philistines' attitude toward Israel and its God changed since 4:7-9?

For Thought and Discussion: a. After being anointed as the future king, how did David try or not try to bring this promise to fulfillment (16:14-17:58)?
b. What implications do you see for Christians either building careers or following callings?

David the warrior (17:1-58)

Champion (17:4). "The ancient Greeks, to whom the Philistines were apparently related, sometimes decided issues of war through chosen champions who met in combat between the armies. Through this economy of warriors the judgment of the gods on the matter at stake was determined. . . . Israel too may have known this practice" (2 Samuel 2:14-16).[1]

Stones (17:40). "Usually the stones chosen were round and smooth and somewhat larger than a baseball. When hurled by a master slinger, they probably traveled at close to 100 miles per hour."[2]

9. How did Goliath's repeated challenges affect Israel's army (17:11,24)?

_____

_____

_____

_____

_____

_____

10. Saul was Israel's giant champion (9:2, 10:23). How had Saul changed since he became king (11:3-8)?

_____

_____

_____

_____

_____

11. We hear David speak for the first time in 17:26. How is his attitude toward the situation different from everyone else's? (See also 17:34-37.)

_____

_____

_____

_____

_____

12. How do Eliab, Saul, and Goliath view David?

17:28 _____

_____

17:33 _____

_____

17:42-44 _____

_____

13. As the Lord said in 16:7, these men looked at the outward appearance. What did the Lord see in David's heart?

_____

_____

_____

_____

_____

14. How does what David said to Saul (17:34-37) and Goliath (17:45-47) indicate that he did *not* look only at the outward appearance?

_____

_____

_____

_____

_____

_____

Optional Application: Do you evaluate people and situations by how they appear outwardly, or do you look deeper and consider them from God's point of view? How can you cultivate the ability to see the heart, as God does?

For Thought and Discussion: What lesson do you see in the contrast between Goliath's and David's weaponry (17:5-7,40)?

Optional Application: David's deep concern for God's honor led him to challenge Goliath. Do you have the courage to speak when you hear others mocking the Lord? How can you do this with love but so that the person(s) involved will be challenged to think?

103

Optional Application: What do David's responses to each of those who criticized, challenged, or mocked him teach you about how you should respond in similar situations?

For Thought and Discussion: Does the story of David and Goliath teach that we should always take up the challenge to defend God's honor? Why or why not?

15. What was it about Goliath that most deeply offended David (17:26,36)?

_____

_____

_____

_____

_____

16. What lesson did David say his victory over Goliath would teach (17:46-47)?

_____

_____

_____

_____

_____

17. This chapter helps explain why God chose David by showing at least one way in which David was "a man after his own heart" (13:14). According to 17:1-58, how did David resemble God?

_____

_____

_____

_____

_____

Whose son is that young man? (17:55). "The seeming contradiction between vv. 55-58 and 16:14-23 may be resolved by noting that prior to this time David was not a permanent resident at Saul's court (see v. 15; 18:2 . . .), so that Saul's knowledge of David and his family may have been minimal. Further, Saul may have been so incredulous at David's courage that he was wondering if his family background and social

104

standing might explain his extraordinary conduct."[3]

Your response

18. What one lesson from 16:1-17:58 would you like to apply to your circumstances?

_____

_____

_____

_____

_____

19. How is this truth relevant to your life? How would you like it to affect your character and actions?

_____

_____

_____

_____

_____

20. What steps can you take to begin doing this?

_____

_____

_____

_____

_____

21. List any questions you have about 16:1-17:58.

_____

_____

_____

_____

Optional Application: Think of some situation or person of concern to you. Are you focused on the outward appearance or on the heart of the matter or person? Pray for God's perspective.

105

For the group

Warm-up. Ask group members to describe times when they have heard someone ridicule the Lord's power, love, or existence. What did they do in response? If no one can think of such a time, ask what they think they would do. You may find it easy to cheer David on in the abstract, but hard to really trust God to intervene powerfully.

An alternate question is, "How is your heart different from your outward appearance?" Ask each person to tell one way he or she is different from the way he or she appears. This exercise will not only help you understand the point of 16:1-17:58, but will also let you get to know each other better.

Questions. This passage is full of thorny issues, but your main focus should be on how David revealed the heart that God saw, the qualities that made God choose him to be king.

Prayer. Praise God for working out His purposes through whatever means are necessary. Praise Him that He often saves not by human effort like sword or spear, but miraculously when someone trusts Him enough to put his life on the line. Praise Him for seeing each of your hearts. Ask Him to give each of you a heart like His, attitudes and perceptions like His and David's.

1. *The NIV Study Bible*, page 400.
2. *The NIV Study Bible*, page 401.
3. *The NIV Study Bible*, page 402.

1 SAMUEL 18:1-20:42

From Favorite to Fugitive

David's skill as therapist and soldier won him Saul's admiration and propelled him to the highest ranks in the nation. But the popular acclaim accorded David served only to arouse the king's suspicion, fear, and finally hatred. These chapters document how David's status changed, through no fault of his own, from Saul's favorite to an outlaw. Yet as his fortunes fluctuated, he enjoyed the unwavering loyalty of a friend who was "closer than a brother."

Saul

Covenant (18:3). This term covered treaties between nations (11:1), contracts between individuals, marriage vows, and pacts between friends. The latter is the thought here. The covenant between God and Israel had elements of a friendship pact and a marriage vow, but it was primarily a treaty between a sovereign and a subject people. Still, the ideas of commitment, loyalty, affection, intimate personal knowledge, and mutual responsibilities run through all covenants.

A covenant could be either bilateral or unilateral; that is, it could be created either by mutual consent or by the will of one party that the other simply accepted. The covenant between Jonathan and David was probably by mutual consent. God's covenant with Israel, however, was due exclusively to His initiative and sustained only through His grace (Deuteronomy 5:2-3, 9:4-29, 10:12-16).

Robe . . . tunic . . . sword . . . bow . . . belt (18:4). The gifts ratified the covenant and symbolized that Jonathan was giving himself to David. The gift of his personal possessions—his clothes and weapons—implies that Jonathan was making David an honorary member of the royal family. They may also suggest that Jonathan recognized that David, not he, would succeed Saul as king (20:14-15).

David his tens of thousands (18:7). Hebrew poetry is structured with parallelism rather than rhyme. Since ten thousand was the customary parallel for one thousand (Deuteronomy 32:30, Psalm 91:7, Micah 6:7), 1 Samuel 18:7 is simply a poetic way of saying "Saul and David have slain thousands." "It is a measure of Saul's insecurity and jealousy that he read [the womens'] intentions incorrectly and took offense. His resentment may have been initially triggered by the mention of David's name alongside his own."[1]

Prophesying (18:10). "The Hebrew for this word is sometimes used to indicate uncontrolled ecstatic behavior . . . and is best understood in that sense in this context."[2] "Prophesying" could also be used of the praise and worship of God under the influence of the Holy Spirit (Numbers 11:24-29; 1 Samuel 10:5,10-11; 19:23). In other situations, it meant the authoritative proclamation of God's word, including comments on the present, instructions for the future, and prediction of the future.

Older daughter (18:17). David was entitled to marry Merab because of his triumph over Goliath (17:25), but now Saul adds more conditions.

No other price (18:25). The father of the bride usually received a sum (Genesis 34:12, Exodus 22:16) "as compensation for the loss of his daughter and insurance for her support if widowed."[3]

Naioth (19:18). The word means "habitations" or "dwellings." It is probably a group of houses in some section of Ramah where a company of prophets lived.[4]

1. What turned Saul, who had previously favored David (16:21-22, 17:55-18:2), against him?

   18:6-9 _____

   _____

   _____

   18:12,15,28-29 _____

   _____

   _____

2. In Saul's fear of and jealousy toward David, to what extent was his thinking accurate and in what sense was it distorted?

   _____

   _____

   _____

   _____

   _____

3. Describe the progression in the tactics Saul used to try to eliminate David.

   18:10-11 _____

   _____

   18:17 _____

   _____

   _____

   18:20-25 _____

   _____

   _____

   _____

19:1-7 _____

_____

_____

19:9-10 _____

_____

19:11-24 _____

_____

_____

_____

_____

4. How did Saul's attitude toward his son Jonathan change, and why (19:1-7, 20:27-33)?

_____

_____

_____

_____

_____

5. What do Saul's tactics and attitudes say about his spiritual condition at this time?

_____

_____

_____

_____

6. The story emphasizes the contrast between Saul and David. What contrasts do you observe in 18:1–20:42?

_____

_____

_____

_____

_____

_____

7. What spiritual lessons are there to be learned
from Saul's enmity toward David?

_____

_____

_____

_____

_____

_____

**For Thought and
Discussion:** What do
you think David
learned through the
difficulties Saul's
opposition made him
suffer? Keep this
question in mind as
you study further in
1 Samuel.

**For Thought and
Discussion:** a. What
does the idea of the
covenant say about
the seriousness of
friendships?
 b. Can you think
of any deep, intimate
friendships in the
New Testament?

Jonathan

New Moon festival (20:5). On the first day of each
 month, Israel consecrated the month to the
 Lord with special sacrifices, blowing trumpets,
 and rest from work (Numbers 10:10, 28:11-15).

Show kindness (20:8,14-15). The definitive way in
 which covenanted people were supposed to treat
 each other was with *hesed*—kindness, loving-
 kindness, steadfast love, mercy, loyalty. This
 word occurs dozens of times in the Old Testament to describe the way God treats His covenant people and the way they are supposed to
 treat Him and each other. David and Jonathan
 had a right to expect *hesed* from each other
 because of the covenant between them. David
 wanted Jonathan to show *hesed* to him by sav-
 ing his life. Jonathan wanted David to do it by
 not wiping out his family when he became king.
 The first ruler of a new dynasty often murdered
 all the rival claimants to the throne from the
 preceeding dynasty, and Jonathan did not want
 this to happen to him and his children. He was
 that convinced that David would be king.
  When the Jews translated their Scriptures

111

Optional Application: Do you find it easy or hard to form committed, intimate friendships? What aspects of your character and lifestyle get in the way? What can you do about them?

Optional Application: To whom can you be the friend Jonathan was to David?

into Greek in 200 BC, they chose the word *agape* ("love") most often as the Greek equivalent of *hesed*. (See the idea of *hesed*, covenant love, behind John 15:12-13.)

Abner (20:25). Saul's cousin and the commander of his army (14:50).

Son of a . . . (20:30). This Hebrew idiom, like its English equivalent, was meant to characterize Jonathan, not his mother.[5]

8. Two of Saul's children sought to help David when Saul turned against him. How does the text emphasize Jonathan as David's most important helper (18:1-4, 19:1-7, 20:1-42)?

_____

_____

_____

_____

_____

_____

_____

9. What irony do you see in the fact that Jonathan became David's closest friend?

_____

_____

_____

_____

_____

10. What does Jonathan's unconcern about inheriting his father's throne (18:4; 20:13-16,31-32) say about his character?

_____

_____

_____

_____

11. What important principles of friendship does Jonathan exemplify in . . .

18:1-4? _____

_____

_____

_____

19:1-7? _____

_____

_____

_____

20:1-42? _____

_____

_____

_____

For Thought and Discussion: The Law commanded the Israelites to love their neighbors as themselves (Leviticus 19:18, 1 Samuel 18:1, Matthew 22:34-40). How does Jonathan demonstrate what this means in 1 Samuel 18:1-20:42?

For Further Study: On the theme of friendship, study Proverbs 14:20; 17:17; 18:24; 19:4,6; 22:11,24; 27:6,10. How are these relevant to your life?

12. Do you think Jonathan and Michal showed due respect toward their father as they sought to protect David? Why or why not?

_____

_____

_____

_____

_____

13. What indications are there in 18:1-20:42 that God was actively watching over David?

_____

_____

_____

For Further Study:
Many of the psalms
were evidently written
by David while Saul
was persecuting him:
5, 6, 13, 18, 22, 25,
26, 27, 28, 31, 35,
40, 52, 54, 55, 56,
57, 58, 59, 62, 63,
64, 69, 70, 71, 86,
109, 142. Read some
of these, and observe
how appropriate they
are to David's situa-
tion. In what ways can
you identify with
David?

**Optional
Application:** Do you
feel afflicted by ene-
mies, or betrayed by
former friends? If so,
read some of David's
psalms written during
this time of his life,
and ask God to care
for you as He cared
for David.

_____

_____

_____

Study Skill—Common Errors in Interpretation
Instead of reading a passage for what God
wants to say through it, people sometimes try
to find in it a message for their current lives
that isn't really there. God's counsel on their
present concerns may be somewhere else in
the Bible, but people are impatient. In lesson
nine you encountered the error of allegoriz-
ing. Two other errors to avoid are:

   1. *Selectivity.* This involves building an
interpretation on certain words and phrases,
while ignoring other phrases and "the overall
sweep of the passage." For instance, there is
a widespread misunderstanding, based on a
few verses in 18:1-20:42, that David and
Jonathan were homosexual lovers. Again, one
could misuse 16:14 to "prove" that God
sends evil spirits to lead people into sin.

   2. *False combination.* This entails com-
bining unconnected elements in a passage
and drawing a conclusion from the
combination.[6]

Your response

14. What aspect of 18:1-20:42 would you like to
    take to heart?

_____

_____

_____

_____

_____

_____

15. How would you like this to affect your life?

_____
_____
_____
_____
_____
_____

16. What can you do to cooperate with God in
bringing this about?

_____
_____
_____
_____

17. List any questions you have about 18:1–20:42.

_____
_____
_____
_____

For the group

Warm-up. Ask everyone to think of his or her closest
friend. Then ask them to think of the greatest act of
friendship that person has shown to him or her. Ask
one or two people to recount their memories.

Prayer. Thank God for your friends. If any of them
have betrayed you, as Saul betrayed David, ask the
Lord to enable you to forgive them and keep trusting Him. You can divide into pairs to pray about
this specifically if necessary. Ask God to help you let
down your barriers and become to someone else the
kind of faithful friend Jonathan was. Ask God to
enable you to overcome any tendency to jealousy or
fear that drives you away from others.

Historical Fiction?

Some scholars think the books of Samuel are more a historical novel than factual history. They point to the large space given to personal and family relationships, comments that purport to indicate God's involvement in the events, moralizing remarks, and so on. They note a lack of emphasis on the social and economic factors that modern historians think are decisive in history. They conclude that the biblical books were really written to edify their readers, rather than to enlighten future generations as to what actually happened.

An evangelical response to such thinking agrees that the supreme purpose of the books of Samuel is not just to inform but to provide spiritual instruction. However, there is no sign that the author invented or even bent the facts to further this aim, nor that he put words in the mouths of the characters. Had he done so, Saul's virtues and David's shortcomings would almost certainly have been eliminated. A secular historian may wonder where the author got his information about exactly what God and men were saying, but these books are called the Former Prophets because their authors were prophets who heard from God.

If the biblical histories do not read like modern history books, it is because of a fundamental difference as to what—or who—really determines history's direction. Both modern and ancient people have seen human history as the chance product of great, impersonal forces. But the biblical writers saw that the chief decider of events is the personal Creator to whom the universe owes its existence. Men, who were created in His image to administer the world, affect history as they respond to or resist His plans. Through the lives of such men as Saul and David we see the difference—for better or worse—that even one individual's life can make.

1. *The NIV Study Bible*, page 403.
2. *The NIV Study Bible*, page 403.
3. *The NIV Study Bible*, pages 403-404.
4. *The NIV Study Bible*, page 405.
5. *The NIV Study Bible*, page 407.
6. Fee and Stuart, page 84.

LESSON ELEVEN

1 SAMUEL 21:1-22:23

Flight and Fury

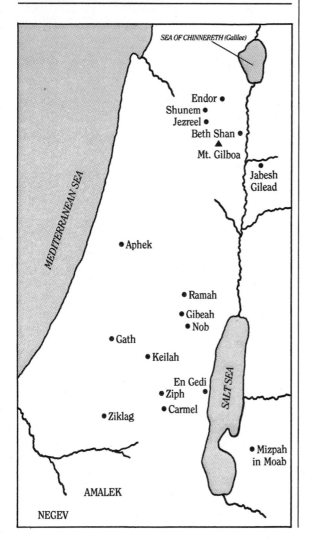

SEA OF CHINNERETH (Galilee)

MEDITERRANEAN SEA

Endor •
Shunem •
Jezreel •
Beth Shan •
▲
Mt. Gilboa

Jabesh
Gilead

• Aphek

• Ramah
• Gibeah
• Nob

• Gath

• Keilah

SALT SEA

En Gedi
• Ziph   •
• Carmel

• Ziklag

• Mizpah
in Moab

AMALEK

NEGEV

For Thought and Discussion: What relationship do you see between the prophecies in 2:27-36, 3:11-14 and what happened to the priests of Nob in 22:18-20?

As Saul's envy hardened into hatred, David was forced to repeatedly avoid and finally abandon the king. In fleeing from Saul, his first stop was the priestly city of Nob. He had no notion of the violence that visit would lead to, the terrible price others would pay for helping him. Read 21:1–22:23.

Deception and bent laws

Nob (21:1). The tabernacle, the table of consecrated bread, some ninety priests, the high priest, and his ephod were all definitely at Nob at this time (21:1,4; 22:17-18,20; 23:6). However, the ark remained at an obscure house in Kiriath Jearim (1 Samuel 7:1, 2 Samuel 6:2-3).

Ahimelech (21:1). Eli's great-grandson, now high priest (14:3, 22:12). Compare 2:31 to 22:18.

Consecrated bread (21:4). "The bread of the Presence" (Exodus 25:30, Leviticus 24:5-9, 1 Samuel 21:6) or "shew bread" (KJV) was twelve loaves that were placed each week in the Holy Place of the tabernacle. They were a thank offering for the provision of daily bread, consecrating the fruit of Israel's labors. "Presence" refers to God's presence as provider and Lord.
   When the week-old loaves were replaced with fresh ones, only the priests could eat them. Ahimelech stretched the law to let David's men have them if the men were ceremonially clean by abstaining from sex (Exodus 19:15, Leviticus 15:18).

1. To obtain food, weapons, and guidance from the Lord (21:3-9, 22:10), David lied to Ahimelech (21:2). He may have been hoping to protect Ahimelech from punishment for knowingly helping Saul's enemy (see 22:13-18). Do you think he was right or wrong to lie? Why?

_____

_____

_____

118

_____

_____

_____

2. To extricate himself from a dangerous situation in Gath, David pretended to be insane (21:10-15). What do you think of this tactic from a moral and spiritual point of view?

_____

_____

_____

_____

_____

3. The Law said only priests could eat the bread of the Presence (Leviticus 24:9). What lesson did Jesus draw from the fact that Ahimelech gave the holy bread to David (Matthew 12:1-8, especially verses 3-4,7)?

_____

_____

_____

_____

4. According to Jesus, is it ever unlawful to do good and save lives (Luke 6:9-10)? Why or why not?

_____

_____

_____

_____

_____

For Thought and Discussion: If you think David was wrong to lie to Ahimelech or the Philistines, what do you think he should have done instead in each case?

Optional Application: Are you in a situation that seems to call for deceit? If so, consider the consequences of David's lie to Ahimelech. What do you think the Lord would have you do in your situation? What might be the consequences of deceit?

5. Were Ahimelech and David wrong to break the ceremonial law? Why or why not?

_____

_____

_____

_____

_____

6. How are this episode in 1 Samuel 21:1-9 and the lessons Jesus draws from it relevant to your life?

_____

_____

_____

_____

_____

David outlawed

Moab (22:3). The Moabites were descendants of Lot, Abraham's nephew (Genesis 19:36-38), and lived east of the Dead Sea. They were usually hostile to Israel (Numbers 22:1-24:25, Judges 3:12-30). David may have been able to find refuge for his parents there because Saul had fought the Moabites (1 Samuel 14:47) and the king of Moab knew of the strife between Saul and David. Also, David's great-grandmother was a Moabitess (Ruth 4:13,22).

7. Which elements of Israelite society associated themselves with David at this time?

22:1-2 _____

_____

22:5 _____

22:20-23 _____

8. Why did these people join David?

_____

_____

_____

_____

9. How did the renegade prophet and priest treat David (22:5,20-23; 23:6-12)?

_____

_____

_____

_____

_____

10. What do your answers to questions 7 through 9 tell you about David?

_____

_____

_____

_____

_____

Saul's vengeance

11. As Saul interrogated his men about David's whereabouts (22:6-8), to what motives did he appeal?

_____

_____

_____

_____

For Thought and Discussion: What significance do you see in David's concern for his parents (22:3-4)?

Optional Application: Although under great pressure and danger, David found time to help others. Ask the Lord to help you notice others' needs and find ways to assist them.

For Further Study: Research the prophet Gad's career in David's service (2 Samuel 24:11-25; 2 Chronicles 29:25,29). What do you learn about a prophet's job in Israel?

12. Compare 22:7 to 8:12,14. What do you observe?

_____

_____

_____

_____

13. When summoned and accused by Saul, how did Ahimelech defend his actions (22:14-15)?

_____

_____

_____

_____

_____

14. In light of Deuteronomy 17:14-20 and 19:15-21, how would you critique Saul's actions in 1 Samuel 22:13-19?

_____

_____

_____

_____

_____

15. a. What contrasts do you see between Saul's treatment of Nob and his actions toward Amalek in chapter 15?

_____

_____

_____

_____

b. What does this difference reveal about Saul's priorities?

_____

_____

_____

_____

For Thought and Discussion: Do events have simple causes or complex ones? What caused the slaughter of the priests of Nob—Eli's sin and God's judgment, David's deceit, Saul's rage, other factors?

16. From your answers to questions 11 through 15, how would you say the monarchy has affected Israel so far? How well is it succeeding?

_____

_____

_____

_____

_____

17. a. To what extent does David admit responsibility for what happened to Nob (22:22)?

_____

_____

b. To what degree would you hold him responsible, and why?

_____

_____

_____

_____

_____

Your response

18. Which truth from 21:1-22:23 strikes you as most personally significant?

_____

_____

_____

123

_____

_____

19. How would you like this to influence your character and actions?

_____

_____

_____

_____

_____

20. What can you do this week along these lines?

_____

_____

_____

_____

_____

21. List any questions you have about 21:1-22:23.

_____

_____

_____

_____

For the group

Warm-up. Ask group members to think of a time when they have lied or misrepresented the truth. What purpose were they trying to achieve? What actually resulted? Don't ask people to answer aloud unless they want to.

Questions. Principles 2 and 3 in the Study Skill on pages 44-45 (lesson three) are both relevant to 21:1-22:23. It is important to evaluate David's, Ahimelech's, and Saul's actions based on eternal moral principles throughout the Scriptures. You may want to choose one or two of the moral dilemmas in these chapters and thoroughly examine what was right or wrong, what should have been done, and how you can apply the same principles in your circumstances. Jesus does this with 21:1-9—would you have drawn the same conclusions on your own?

Prayer. Thank God for getting His will accomplished in spite of imperfect people like David and Saul. Ask Him to show you what He wants each of you to do in your various difficult situations.

1 SAMUEL 23:1-24:22

Trust and Respect

David flees for his life and Saul devotes his energy and the resources of his realm to pursuing him. More than once David escapes, but with every sunrise he finds that the territory within which he can move is diminished. This is a time of testing and training for David, as God teaches him about Himself and molds him into His image. Read 23:1-24:22.

1. Chapters 16 through 31 form the fourth section of 1 Samuel. Below is a half-completed outline of the book. Fill in titles in the blank spaces for chapters 16 through 22. (If you prefer, you can use another sheet of paper and your outlines on pages 55 and 94. You can make up titles for chapters 23 through 31 either now or after finishing lesson fifteen.)

   (1:1-7:17) The Stage Is Set for the Establishment of the Kingship.
      (1:1-3:21) The birth and calling of the prophet responsible for the transition; judgment upon Eli's house for its performance in the last era.
      (4:1-7:17) God displays His (and His prophet's) holiness and competence to rule through Israel's defeat and victory.
   (8:1-12:25) God Establishes the Kingship through Samuel's Work.
      (8:1-22) The people's sinful motives for wanting a king, and God's response.

127

(9:1–10:16) Samuel anoints Saul privately.
(10:17-27) Saul chosen by lot publicly.
(11:1-13) Saul confirmed by a military
victory.
(11:14–12:25) Saul's reign inaugurated at a
covenant renewal ceremony.
(13:1–15:35) Saul Fails the Tests of a Good
King.
(13:1-15) Craven disobedience.
(13:16–14:52) A rash and arrogant oath.
(15:1-35) Craven disobedience.

(16:1–31:13) _____

_____

_____

(16:1-13) _____

_____

_____

(16:14-23) _____

_____

_____

(17:1-58) _____

_____

_____

(18:1–20:42) _____

_____

_____

_____

(21:1–22:23) _____

_____

_____

_____

(23:1-26:25) _____

_____

_____

_____

(27:1-29:11) _____

_____

_____

_____

(30:1-31:13) _____

_____

_____

_____

For Thought and Discussion: a. What prompted David to intervene on Keilah's behalf?

b. How might what happened to Nob have affected David's decision to leave Keilah?

For Thought and Discussion: a. What role did God's promises play in David's life at this time (23:15-18, 25:28-31)?

b. How do God's promises affect your experience, attitudes, and decisions?

At Keilah and Ziph (23:1-29)

Looting the threshing floors (23:1). The Philistines apparently waited until after the Israelites had harvested the wheat and finished the laborious task of threshing (separating the grain from the stalks on which it had grown). Then they would come and carry off just the grain by force. Thus, the Israelites would have nothing to show for all their work.

The ephod (23:6). The high priest's ephod with the Urim and Thummim for asking yes-or-no questions of the Lord. See pages 65 and 84.

2. What is the point about the story of David and Keilah (23:1-6)? What does it say about David and God?

_____

_____

_____

129

For Thought and Discussion: a. Why were the people of Keilah and Ziph willing to give David to Saul (23:12,19-20)? Are you surprised?

b. Do you think they were wrong to obey their king in this matter? Why or why not?

For Thought and Discussion: What is Jonathan's attitude about being second to David (23:17)? How is he a model for us?

For Thought and Discussion: a. Why do you think God wanted David to experience such difficulties?

b. Does He have the same purposes for problems in Christians' lives? Explain.

Optional Application: a. Can you trust the Lord to take care of you the way He took care of David? Why or why not?

b. How should your actions reflect your convictions?

Six hundred (23:13). The number has increased since 22:2.

3. How is David sustained and helped in his flight from Saul in chapter 23?

23:9-13 _____

23:14 _____

23:15-18 _____

23:19-29 _____

4. What do these events demonstrate about the Lord?

130

David spares Saul's life (24:1-22)

5. How does David get a chance to kill Saul at En Gedi (24:1-3)?

_____

_____

_____

_____

_____

6. In what way does David's theological principle differ from his men's (24:4-7)?

_____

_____

_____

_____

_____

7. What practical difference does this disagreement in theological principles make?

_____

_____

_____

_____

_____

8. Summarize David's words to Saul in 24:8-15.

_____

_____

_____

_____

_____

For Thought and Discussion: a. Do you think you would have let Saul live? Why or why not?
    b. What was David risking, and what did he hope to gain, by saving Saul?

131

For Thought and Discussion: a. Did David spare Saul's life out of a general forgiving attitude, or did he have other reasons? Explain.

b. Do David's reasons for sparing Saul apply to any situation you are in? Explain.

Optional Application: Are you at odds with anyone in authority over you? How can you show the kind of submission David showed even a mad king like Saul (24:5-15)?

9. Why is 24:12,15 important? What does it say about David and God?

_____

_____

_____

_____

_____

10. What are the important points of Saul's reply to David (24:16-21)?

_____

_____

_____

_____

_____

Your response

11. What can we learn about what it means to be a man after God's heart from 23:1-24:22?

_____

_____

_____

_____

_____

_____

_____

12. What one insight from 23:1-24:22 would you like to take to heart personally?

132

_____

_____

_____

_____

_____

13. How would you like this insight to affect your character and attitudes?

_____

_____

_____

_____

_____

14. What action can you take to put this into practice this week?

_____

_____

_____

_____

15. List any questions you have about 23:1–24:22.

_____

_____

_____

_____

For the group

Warm-up. Ask group members to evaluate silently how close they are to someone in spiritual authority over them. How much respect do they have for that person? Then ask them to recall the last time they did something to show their respect for and submission to that person. No one needs to respond aloud unless he wants to; you can discuss this after you've looked at how David treated his king who was mad and out to kill him.

Questions. Chapter 23 basically outlines how God consistently protected David in his flight from Saul. Chapter 24 recounts how David spared Saul not because he deserved it as a man or because David was an especially forgiving person, but because David respected Saul's office as from the Lord. You can focus on either or both of these topics. How have you fallen short either in trusting God to take care of you or in respecting people because the Lord put them over you? How have you succeeded in doing these things? What opportunities do you have this week to put either or both of these into practice? Be open in sharing with each other your real failings, successes, and situations.

Prayer. Ask the Lord to help you become serious about trusting Him and respecting those over you. Pray especially about any situations in which any of you are struggling to trust God or to respect a leader who seems ungodly or unwise. Thank God for having your lives under control, despite appearances.

1 SAMUEL 25:1-26:25

Returning Good for Evil

David spared Saul's life at En Gedi primarily because he respected the office of the Lord's anointed (24:6). He claimed to trust that the Lord would avenge him if he stayed in submission to Saul (24:12,15). But does David think he owes such forbearance only to his superior? Does he really understand the implications of God's words: "It is mine to avenge; I will repay" (Deuteronomy 32:35)? Read 25:1-26:25.

David, Nabal, and Abigail (25:1-44)

Sheep-shearing time . . . a festive time (25:7-8). The counting of the sheep before shearing "would have shown how well the flocks had fared during the recent grazing," and shearing meant income soon. "David was hoping that Nabal would be in a mood to repay past favours."[1] David and his men had protected Nabal's sheep from pillage during the grazing months (25:7,15-16,21).

1. Summarize what happens in 25:1-44.

_____

_____

_____

For Thought and Discussion: Is the Lord opposed only to revenge against those over you, or to revenge in general? What is the evidence of 1 Samuel 25?

For Further Study: Research what the Scripture says about how we should regard and treat our "enemies" (Exodus 23:4-5, Leviticus 19:17-18, Deuteronomy 32:35, Matthew 5:43-48, Romans 12:19, Hebrews 10:30). What does God say about revenge?

2. How would you describe Nabal's character from 25:10-11?

_____

_____

_____

3. In what ways is Nabal like Saul in the way he treats David (25:10-11,14-17,21)?

_____

_____

_____

_____

4. What other subtle signs are there that Nabal is being compared to Saul?

25:25 (compare 26:21) _____

_____

25:36 _____

_____

5. How did David plan to deal with Nabal (25:12,21-22)?

_____

_____

_____

_____

_____

136

6. What does this reveal about David's natural inclinations when wronged?

_____

_____

_____

_____

7. Why was it a blessing for David that Abigail dissuaded him from his plans (25:26-34)?

_____

_____

_____

_____

_____

8. What was it about Abigail that you think caused David to marry her?

_____

_____

_____

_____

_____

For Thought and Discussion: What does even an obscure woman like Abigail know about David (25:28-29)? What are the implications of this?

For Thought and Discussion: Do you think Abigail's actions are intended as a model for Christians in general or for Christian wives in particular? Why or why not?

Optional Application: Abigail probably prevented David from doing to Nabal's household what Saul did to Nob. Do you have the necessary courage, humility, and love to confront other believers in danger of committing serious mistakes? Pray about whether there is anyone you need to confront.

David spares Saul again (26:1-25)

Accept an offering (26:19). David suggests that if he has unknowingly wronged Saul, let the matter be settled between him and God, without Saul taking personal revenge.

The LORD's inheritance (26:19). This is a key concept in the Old Testament. It includes both the Lord's people and His land (Exodus 15:17, 34:9). David has been excluded from fellowship with God's people and enjoyment of His land. Even worse, the Israelites believed that to be

For Thought and Discussion: a. What evidence does David give in 25:1-26:25 of reverence for the Lord, respect for the king, and humility about himself?

b. Is it possible to develop one of these qualities without the rest? Explain.

Optional Application: How can you cultivate and act with reverence for God, respect for His people, and humility toward yourself this week?

For Further Study: Compare David's act of forgiveness to Matthew 6:12-15, 18:15-35; Ephesians 4:32; Colossians 3:13. What example and incentives do we have to forgive others that is even greater than David had?

expelled from the place of God's tabernacle and lawful sacrifices doomed a man to worship the gods of whatever land he settled in.[2]

9. How is the situation in chapter 26 like and unlike the one in chapter 24?

like _____

_____

_____

_____

_____

_____

_____

unlike _____

_____

_____

_____

_____

_____

Abishai (26:6). David's nephew (1 Chronicles 2:16).

10. Like David's men the last time (24:4), Abishai assumes that God has delivered Saul to David so that David can kill him (26:8). Why does David refuse to kill the king (26:9-11)?

_____

_____

_____

_____

138

11. Why do you think God twice gave David a chance to kill Saul? (Consider what David and Saul say to each other in 26:17-25, and what you observed about David in 25:1-44.)

_____

_____

_____

_____

_____

Your response

12. How does David further show himself to be a man after God's heart in 25:1-26:25?

_____

_____

_____

_____

_____

_____

_____

_____

13. What truth from 25:1-26:25 would you like to apply to your own life this week?

_____

_____

_____

_____

_____

_____

14. How have you already seen this truth active in your life?

_____

_____

_____

_____

_____

_____

15. How would you like it to affect your character and habits in deeper ways?

_____

_____

_____

_____

_____

16. What steps can you take this week toward bringing this about?

_____

_____

_____

_____

_____

_____

17. List any questions you have about 25:1-26:25.

_____

_____

_____

_____

For the group

Warm-up. Ask the group, "Think of a time in the last week when you have had a choice whether to forgive or get even. What did you do?" Group members don't need to recount the situations, just tell whether or not they chose to forgive. Ask them to search their hearts to see whether they really have forgiven.

Questions. The story of Nabal sheds light on David's chances to kill Saul. Clearly, forgiveness and refusal to retaliate did not come naturally to David. Share some of your own struggles to forgive.

Prayer. Thank God for the examples of David and Abigail. Ask Him to help you forgive those who have wronged you, no matter how many times they show empty remorse and do the same thing all over again. Pray to have His ceaselessly forgiving heart. Pray about specific situations in group members' lives if necessary.

Doublets

In the biblical narrative books, events often recur that are very similar to one another. For instance, Abraham twice deceives people into thinking that his wife is his sister, and his son Isaac does this same thing once (Genesis 12, 20, 26). In 1 Samuel, David twice spares Saul's life. These parallels have led some scholars to conclude that single events were multiplied by the books' authors and editor into repeated ones.

However, similarity between events is not grounds to deny their historicity. History knows of many instances in which similar events recurred. Athanasius, the Christian theologian, suffered exile some five times, and Napoleon Bonaparte twice. The biblical writers carefully selected and ordered the events they described so as to highlight the lessons they perceived in those events. Sometimes, similar events are recorded so as to emphasize that this was a recurring pattern (such as the habitual sin of Abraham passed on to his son). At other times, similar events teach slightly contrasting lessons.

(continued on page 142)

141

(continued from page 141)

The author of 1 Samuel brilliantly sandwiched the story of Nabal between two instances of David forgiving Saul. Together, they show how David had to learn to forgive repeatedly, to forbear revenge against the Lord's anointed and against ordinary men. They also show how Saul did not learn from repeated demonstrations of David's loyalty. Whenever you encounter doublets, think about what each incident teaches individually and what they teach together.

1. Gordon, page 182.
2. *The NIV Study Bible*, page 414.

1 SAMUEL 27:1-29:11

The Philistines as Friend and Foe

Although David has twice spared Saul's life, and in spite of promises to the contrary, the king continues to pursue him. So, despairing of any real change in Saul, David decides to abandon his homeland and settle in Philistia. This could spell disaster, but read 27:1-29:11.

David in Philistia (27:1-12, 28:1-3, 29:1-11)

Geshurites . . . Girzites . . . Amalekites (27:8). Three pagan groups whom Israel failed to conquer under Joshua (Joshua 13:1-3). Exterminating the pagans conformed to the instructions God gave Moses and Joshua (Deuteronomy 7:1-2, Joshua 6:21), although David did it for other reasons as well (1 Samuel 27:11).

Negev of . . . (27:10). David told Achish that he was raiding Israelites, when he was really raiding their enemies.

You must understand (28:1). "In the ancient Near East, to accept sanctuary in a country involved obligations of military service."[1]

1. Do you think David's move into Philistine territory reflects a lack of faith in the Lord (27:1)? Why or why not?

For Thought and Discussion: a. Does the Scripture suggest that David was right to leave Israel rather than split the nation over a contest between him and Saul? Why or why not?

b. Study some New Testament situations in which separation is shown to be preferable to conflict (Acts 15:36-41, 1 Corinthians 7:10-11). Does this apply to any situation you are facing?

For Thought and Discussion: a. How were David's words to Achish consistently ambiguous and deceptive (28:2, 29:8)?

b. Whom do you think David really meant by "my lord the king" (29:8)?

c. What do you think of David's policy of deception in a desperate and dangerous situation?

Optional Application: Had certain Philistine leaders not objected, David might have found himself forced to fight against his own people. Are you entangled in commitments that could force you to make spiritual compromises or betray someone? On the other hand, are you known among Christians and nonChristians as a person who keeps his word?

2. Why do you suppose David now felt comfortable moving to Gath (27:2-3), although previously he had feared for his life there (21:10-15)? What had changed?

3. How did David support himself while living in Achish's territory (27:8-9)?

4. Why did David lie to Achish about his activities (27:10-12)?

5. What was the result of David's move to Philistia (28:1-2, 29:1-11)?

144

_____
_____
_____
_____
_____
_____

6. How did David escape this dilemma (29:1-11)?

_____
_____
_____
_____
_____

7. a. How did the actions of Abigail (25:18-31) and Achish (29:6-11) affect David in similar ways?

_____
_____
_____
_____

b. What do their interventions into David's actions show about God?

_____
_____
_____
_____

Saul's desperation (28:3-25)

8. What problems did Saul face at this time (28:3-6)?

_____
_____

For Thought and Discussion: If it were against the law to be a Christian, would you lie to the authorities about your faith or activities? Why or why not?

For Thought and Discussion: Does God graciously intervene in the lives of Christians as He did in David's life to prevent him from sinning (25:18-31, 29:6-11)? Have you experienced this? Explain.

Optional Application: God cared for David while in foreign territory and guarded him from sinning because he genuinely wanted to seek God's honor and His people's good. Can you rely on God's care and guarding in your own life? What should you do in light of this?

145

Optional Application: Saul sought the Lord's will too late, after disobeying it too often when he knew it. Does your obedience tend to be immediate or delayed, complete or partial? Think and pray about some recent examples.

For Further Study: How does a Christian inquire of the Lord? What methods are permitted and forbidden? Research answers in the Bible.

For Thought and Discussion: Why does the Lord detest mediums and spiritists?

_____
_____
_____
_____

Dreams or Urim or prophets (28:6). Saul sought guidance from the Lord both by personal revelation and by the agency of priests and prophets. David had a prophet, but no prophet served Saul. Likewise, David's priest Abiathar had the ephod with the Urim and Thummin. Saul may have had copies of the lots made, or the author of 1 Samuel may be speaking idiomatically of the three usual ways of inquiring of the Lord.

9. What did Saul do when God refused to speak to him (28:7-15)?

_____
_____
_____
_____
_____
_____

Saul had expelled the mediums and spiritists from the land (28:3). This may mean he'd had them executed unless they managed to flee the country (see 28:9,21). The Law commanded that occult practitioners be executed (Leviticus 19:31; 20:6,27; Deuteronomy 18:11).

    This statement illustrates that much more happened during Saul's reign than is included in the books of Samuel (compare 2 Samuel 21:1-2). The author selected only those details that were essential to the themes God wanted to convey.

10. Why do you think Saul sought to contact Samuel?

_____

_____

_____

_____

_____

For Further Study:
Compare what Samuel says to Saul in chapter 28 to what the Lord revealed to Eli through Samuel in chapter 3. What similarities do you see? Does this say something about the Lord?

11. What message did Samuel deliver to Saul (28:16-19)?

_____

_____

_____

_____

_____

12. How did Saul react to Samuel's words (28:20-25)?

_____

_____

_____

_____

_____

13. What does this whole episode, including Saul's final reaction, reveal about his psychological and spiritual state?

_____

_____

_____

_____

_____

This strange passage is the only biblical occurrence of someone coming back from the grave without having been resurrected. Many readers wonder how a witch or medium could have the power and authority to really call someone up from the dead. Did God permit Samuel's spirit to speak to Saul? Did the woman contact some other good or evil spirit that pretended to be Samuel? Did she telepathically discern and conjure up an image from Saul's thoughts? And finally, what light, if any, does this shed on the claims of modern mediums?

To understand this incident, it is essential to note what is said and reflect on the author's purpose. First, the text says that it was Samuel (28:15) and that Saul recognized him for who he was (28:14). Second, Samuel basically repeated what he had previously told the king about God's judgment on him (28:16-19; compare 13:13-14, 15:10-29). Third, the only new elements were that on the following day, Israel would be defeated and Saul and his sons would be killed in battle. These prophecies were fulfilled (28:19, 31:1-7).

It seems that the author of 1 Samuel did not intend to suggest that mediums should be consulted or that they had any real power over the dead. (The account says nothing about the woman doing anything to bring up Samuel, and she plays no part in his dialogue with Saul.) Nor did he mean to teach concerning the state of the dead. Rather, his exclusive interest was in reaffirming God's judgment on Saul and His choice of David as the next king. We may find God's method of reaffirming these things unorthodox, but guessing about matters God did not choose to explain generally leads to confusion.

Your response

14. What aspect of 27:1–29:11 would you most like to take to heart?

_____

_____

_____

_____

_____

15. How would you like this to influence your character and habits?

_____

_____

_____

_____

16. What steps can you take to begin this process?

_____

_____

_____

_____

17. List any questions you have about 27:1–29:11.

_____

_____

_____

_____

For the group

Warm-up. Ask group members how they go about finding out what the Lord wants them to do. Just go around the room, giving everyone a minute or so to answer.

Questions. When you discuss 27:1–29:11, connect the group's responses to the warm-up with the situations in the text. Do you think David would have gone to Gath if he had been listening to God? What would Saul have done differently if he'd had a lifestyle of listening to and obeying God? Why did David's sojourn in Gath, despite deceit and a risk of disloyalty, cause no disaster, while Saul's fear and consequent sin brought catastrophe? (This last is a tough question; you may not resolve it.)

You may have discussed David's tendency toward deceit earlier. If so, ask whether group members have been more aware of their own temptations to distort the truth, and whether they have been able to resist. If the group is interested, suggest that someone research biblical passages about lying, deceit, and falsehood to answer the question, "Can deceit ever be justified, even to save lives?" A concordance will yield dozens of references to *lie(s), deceit, falsehood, true/truth, honest(y)*, and so on. Ask the researcher to report back next week with his or her findings.

Don't spend time debating what really happened at the medium's house in Endor. Instead, discuss why God hates mediums and magic, and how He wants His people to find out what to do. How disciplined and effective are you at listening to God? How can you become more disciplined? Persistent prayer, Bible study, and fellowship are absolutely essential for avoiding delusion; there just aren't any shortcuts.

Prayer. Thank God for protecting David from sin and danger while in flight from Saul. Praise His awesome justice and abhorrence of all rebellious prying into knowledge He has hidden. Ask Him to teach you to listen accurately and diligently to Him, and to guide you in obeying Him. Ask Him to guard each of you from sin as He guarded David.

1. *The NIV Study Bible*, page 416.

LESSON FIFTEEN

1 SAMUEL 30:1-31:13

Victory and Death

Saul has hit the bottom of the spiritual pit into
which he has been plunging. He has consulted a
medium and has been promised death today. David
has narrowly escaped joining the Philistines in shat-
tering Israel and decimating Saul's family. The final
act is at hand. Read 30:1-31:13.

David and Amalek (30:1-31)

1. In David's absence, the Amalekites seized the
   chance to take revenge for raids they had suffered. Why did this attack devastate David's men
   (30:1-4)?

   _____

   _____

   _____

   _____

2. Why was David's own situation especially desperate (30:5-6)?

   _____

   _____

   _____

   _____

For Further Study:
Compare David's trial
(1 Samuel 30:6) to
Moses' (Numbers
14:1-10). Have you
ever seen this happen
to a Christian leader?
Pray that your leaders
find strength to han-
dle this in the Lord.

**Optional
Application:** David
had a priest to seek
God's will for him
(30:7-8). What
resources does God
offer you as you face
practical decisions in
your life? Are you
making use of all of
them?

151

3. How was David able to keep going and overcome this crisis (30:6)?

_____

_____

_____

_____

_____

4. How did the outcome of this affair further strengthen David's position as the heir to the throne (30:16-20)?

_____

_____

_____

_____

5. How did the aftermath of this battle reveal David's theology and sense of justice (30:21-25)?

_____

_____

_____

_____

_____

6. What does 30:1-31 demonstrate about David's character? In what ways does he act as a man after God's heart?

_____

_____

_____

_____

_____

7. What does chapter 30 say once again about God?

_____

_____

_____

_____

Saul's death (31:1-13)

8. In his last battle with the Philistines, what tragedies did Saul witness before his death (31:1-2)?

_____

_____

_____

_____

9. How did Saul die (31:3-6)?

_____

_____

_____

10. What do you think the author of 1 Samuel (and the Holy Spirit) wanted to emphasize about Saul in the account of how he died?

_____

_____

_____

_____

_____

11. a. Why did the citizens of Jabesh Gilead risk their lives to recover Saul's body and bury his bones (31:11-13)? Recall 11:1-11.

_____

Optional Application: a. How did Saul's unfaithfulness affect his family? How did his passion to have his son inherit affect that son? (Compare Exodus 20:4-6.)

b. Who else bears the cost of your sin? What might happen to your family if you put ambition ahead of the Lord's will? What should you do about this?

For Thought and Discussion: a. Compare the Philistines' treatment of Saul's corpse (31:9-10) to 17:51. What do you learn?

b. Do you see any symbolic significance in the fact that Saul was decapitated? Explain.

For Further Study:
Saul's fear of being captured alive by the Philistines may reflect his knowledge of how they treated Samson (Judges 16:18-27).

For Thought and Discussion: What does chapter 31 reveal about Israel's request for a king in chapter 8?

_____

_____

_____

b. What does this act say about them?

_____

_____

_____

_____

12. How does Israel's situation at the end of chapter 13 compare with that at the end of chapter 4?

_____

_____

_____

_____

13. What were the consequences of Saul's reign for Israel?

_____

_____

_____

_____

_____

14. What contrasts do these two final chapters of 1 Samuel present?

_____

_____

_____

_____

_____

154

15. Go back to page 129 and fill in the rest of the outline of 1 Samuel.

Your response

16. What aspect of 30:1–31:13 would you like to take to heart?

_____

_____

_____

_____

_____

17. How would you like this to affect you?

_____

_____

_____

_____

_____

18. What action can you take to put this into practice this week?

_____

_____

_____

_____

_____

19. List any questions you have about 30:1–31:13.

_____

_____

_____

_____

For the group

Warm-up. Ask each person to recall a time when circumstances brought him or her to the brink of despair. Let as many as possible tell briefly what the situation was, and what they did. Bringing up these memories will help you identify with David's situation in chapter 30 and compare your reactions to his.

Prayer. Praise God that He faithfully fulfills His promises for blessing and judgment. Thank Him that you can rely on Him absolutely in the worst disaster. Ask Him to help each of you take seriously and act in light of the awful consequences of Saul's rebellion. Ask Him to help you live in view of the joyful consequences of David's trust.

Artificial Divisions

The division of the books of the Bible into chapters and verses makes it much easier to locate specific passages in the text. However, it often obscures the wholeness of the narratives. For instance, the books of Samuel, Kings, Chronicles, and Luke-Acts were all originally written as single works. (Samuel and Kings seem originally to have been one work.[1]) Samuel was divided in the Greek Old Testament about 200 BC and in the Hebrew Old Testament about 1400 AD.[2] The Old Testament chapter and verse divisions were also devised around 200 AD.

So, no study of 1 Samuel is complete without some reference to the beginning of 2 Samuel, in which we learn about the strife Israel suffered after Saul's death. And we will fully understand its message only as we are familiar with Joshua, Judges, and Kings, which together give the entire biblical perspective on the period of Israel's rise and fall. As you study Scripture, remember to allow the flow of its narratives, rather than artificial verse and chapter divisions, to control your reading and reflection.

---

1. *The New Bible Dictionary*, second edition, page 659.
2. *The New Bible Dictionary*, page 1066.

REVIEW

After studying 1 Samuel passage by passage, it is important to look back at the entire book. This lesson is intended to help you understand truths that emerge as you consider 1 Samuel as a whole.

Study Skill—Charts and Diagrams

An outline as you have worked on (pages 55, 94, 128-129) is a great help in pulling a book together. Another useful tool is a chart that makes a picture of the book (or some aspect) that can be taken in at a glance.

On pages 158 and 159 you will find two charts that look like empty graphs. The horizontal axis (the line that goes left to right) of each graph measures 1 Samuel from chapter 1 to chapter 31. The vertical axis (the line that goes bottom to top) measures growth and decline in the lives of the main characters of the book. The life of Samuel is graphed on each chart as an example for you; the line goes up when his power or spirituality grows, and vice versa. Use two different colors to draw lines for the lives of Saul and David on each chart.

---

1. Trace the rise and fall of the *power or influence* of each of the book's three leading figures.

2. Trace the growth and decline of these men *spiritually.*

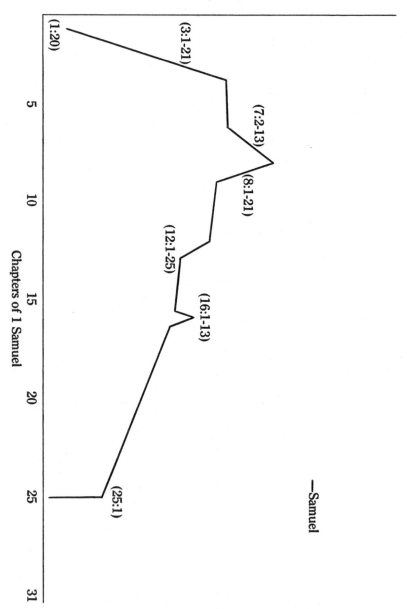

Power/Influence

(1:20)

(3:1-21)

(7:2-13)

(8:1-21)

(12:1-25)

(16:1-13)

(25:1)

5

10

15

20

25

31

Chapters of 1 Samuel

—Samuel

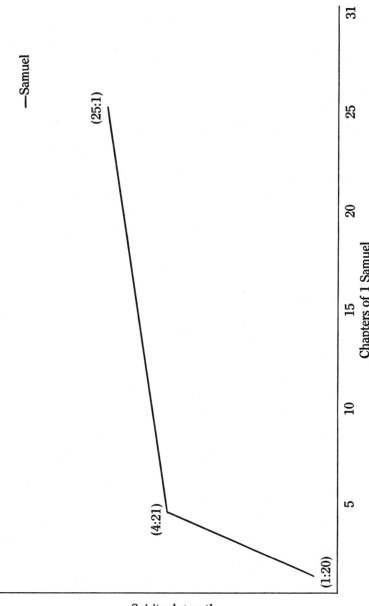

Spiritual growth

Chapters of 1 Samuel

—Samuel

(1:20)

(4:21)

(25:1)

3. What lessons or conclusions can you draw from these two charts? What do they reveal about the themes of the book?

_____

_____

_____

_____

_____

_____

4. In 16:7, God says, "Man looks at the outward appearance, but God looks at the heart." How did Saul exemplify the kind of man who appeared to be good king material (9:2,21; 11:1-11)?

_____

_____

_____

_____

_____

5. What traits did Saul show that made him unfit to be king (13:7-12; 14:24,38-46; 15:1-35; 17:10-11; 18:6-29; 19:1-24; 20:27-33; 22:6-19; 24:16-21; 26:21-25; 28:5-25; 31:1-6)?

_____

_____

_____

_____

_____

_____

_____

_____

6. How did David show himself to be the kind of man God wanted to rule His people, a man after God's heart (16:14-23; 17:26-58; 18:18,23-27; 20:1-42; 22:3-4,20-23; 23:1-6; 24:1-22; 25:1-44; 26:1-25; 30:1-31)?

_____

_____

_____

_____

_____

_____

_____

_____

7. Did Israel progress, regress, or remain static politically and religiously during the period covered in 1 Samuel? Explain why you think so.

_____

_____

_____

_____

_____

_____

8. What picture of God do you get from 1 Samuel? (*Optional:* Think about 1:27; 2:1-11,17,27-36; 3:11-21; 4:10; 5:1-12; 6:12,19-20; 7:3; 8:7-22; 10:9-10; 11:6-11; 12:8-25; 13:11-14; 14:15,36-45; 15:11,22-23,26-29; 16:7,14; 17:45-47; 18:12-14; 19:18-24; 22:18; 23:9-12,26-29; 24:6,12; 28:15-19; 29:6-7; 30:6-8.)

_____

_____

_____

For Further Study: How does Jesus in the gospels show even more brightly the qualities that made David a man after God's heart?

For Thought and Discussion: Which of the minor characters in 1 Samuel seems most significant to you as a positive or negative example?

For Thought and Discussion: a. Which aspects of God's character challenged you the most as you studied 1 Samuel?
b. Was there anything about the portrayal of the Lord that troubled you?

For Further Study:
Trace through
1 Samuel the themes
of life and death, vic-
tory and defeat, and
faithfulness and dis-
obedience. How do
these work together
to reinforce the basic
message of the
book?

**For Thought and
Discussion:** How
does the impact of
individuals on Israel's
history, for better or
worse, affect your
feelings about your
significance in today's
world?

**For Thought and
Discussion:** What
has your time in
1 Samuel taught you
about studying large
portions of God's
Word as opposed to
concentrating on
short passages and
familiar verses?

9. What spiritual lessons from 1 Samuel seem most important to you personally?

_____

_____

_____

_____

_____

10. How have you changed as a result of your study of 1 Samuel?

_____

_____

_____

_____

11. Look back at questions in which you expressed a desire to make some application. Are you sat-isfied with your follow-through? If there are any matters you want to continue to focus on or actions you want to pursue, write them down.

_____

_____

_____

_____

_____

_____

_____

12. Check the end of each lesson to see if any of
    your questions remain unanswered. If so, write
    them here, and plan how to seek answers.
    Research in one of the books on pages 165-168,
    or ask some Christian whose maturity and bibli-
    cal knowledge you trust.

_____

_____

_____

_____

_____

For the group

Reviewing a book can be vague and general because
people remember it only dimly or have difficulty
tying details together to see the big picture. Review
can also be a dull rehash of what people feel they
have already learned.

On the other hand, it can be an exciting
chance to see the story as God sees it, as a whole.
The keys to achieving this latter situation are the
attitudes of the leader and the group. The leader
needs to motivate the group to want to see the
God's-eye view. He or she needs to encourage
members who find it hard to connect ideas from
many chapters. He or she must also urge the group
to think deeply when quick answers seem to say
everything easily. At the same time, each group
member needs to discipline himself to think and
pray more deeply.

Warm-up. It might be motivating to ask, "What is
the most exciting thing you have learned about God
from studying 1 Samuel?"

Questions. Try to split your time evenly between
reviewing the content of the book (questions 1

through 8) and assessing how you have applied and want to apply it (questions 9-11). Also give everyone a chance to ask about anything they still don't understand (question 12). Encourage group members, rather than the leader, to suggest or find answers so that the group will grow less dependent on the leader.

Dividing your time like this may mean that you will not be able to discuss all the content questions in equal depth. However, if everyone has prepared answers, it should be easy to get rich pictures of Saul, David, and God in five or ten minutes each.

Compare your charts from questions 1 and 2. Are you in general agreement? What relationship do you see between Saul's spiritual rise and fall and the rise and fall of his power?

When you review applications, try not to let members compare their growth to each other's or to focus on guilt and failure. If anyone feels he has not obeyed God or grown much, you can discuss whether that is true and how the person can approach the situation from now on. Strive to encourage one another.

Evaluation. You might set aside a whole meeting to evaluate your study of 1 Samuel and plan where to go next. Here are some questions you might consider:

> How well did the study help you grasp the book of 1 Samuel?
> What did you like best about your meetings?
> What did you like least? What would you change, and how?
> How well did you meet the goals you set at your first meeting?
> What did you learn about small group study?
> How could you practice together something you learned from your study?
> What are the members' current needs? What will you do next?

Worship. Praise God for revealing Himself to you through the book of 1 Samuel. Thank Him for what He is doing in each of your lives. Ask Him to guide you as to where you should go from here.

STUDY AIDS

For further information on the material covered in this study, consider the following sources. If your local bookstore does not have them, ask the bookstore to order them from the publisher, or find them in a seminary library. Many university and public libraries also carry these books.

Commentaries on 1 Samuel

Gordon, Robert P. *1 and 2 Samuel* (Paternoster Press, 1986).
> Gordon, an evangelical, is a lecturer in Old Testament at Cambridge University. His commentary communicates his own thorough knowledge of the Hebrew text of 1 and 2 Samuel clearly and concisely. He is careful not to read anything into these books that is not there, nor to leave anything out of them that is, but rather concentrates on their original, basic meaning. This commentary does not require any knowledge of Hebrew to be used effectively, and is probably the best choice for a first commentary on Samuel.

Klein, Ralph W. *1 Samuel* (Word Books, 1983).
> Klein's work is based on his own translation of the Hebrew text and includes extensive discussions of technical issues. He does provide detailed comments on each portion of the book that do not require any knowledge of Hebrew to understand, but on the whole this is more of an "advanced" work than Gordon's.

Histories, Concordances, Dictionaries, and Handbooks

A *history* or *survey* traces Israel's history from beginning to end, so that you can see where each biblical event fits. *A Survey of Israel's History* by Leon Wood (Zondervan, 1970) is a good basic introduction for laymen from a con-

165

servative viewpoint. Not critical or heavily learned, but not simplistic. Many other good histories are available.

A *concordance* lists words of the Bible alphabetically along with each verse in which the word appears. It lets you do your own word studies. An *exhaustive* concordance lists every word used in a given translation, while an *abridged* or *complete* concordance omits either some words, some occurrences of the word, or both.

The two best exhaustive concordances are *Strong's Exhaustive Concordance* and *Young's Analytical Concordance to the Bible*. Both are available based on the King James Version of the Bible and the New American Standard Bible. *Strong's* has an index by which you can find out which Greek or Hebrew word is used in a given English verse. *Young's* breaks up each English word it translates. However, neither concordance requires knowledge of the original language.

Among other good, less expensive concordances, *Cruden's Complete Concordance* is keyed to the King James and Revised Versions, and *The NIV Complete Concordance* is keyed to the New International Version. These include all references to every word included, but they omit "minor" words. They also lack indexes to the original languages.

A **Bible dictionary** or **Bible encyclopedia** alphabetically lists articles about people, places, doctrines, important words, customs, and geography of the Bible.

The New Bible Dictionary, edited by J. D. Douglas, F. F. Bruce, J. I. Packer, N. Hillyer, D. Guthrie, A. R. Millard, and D. J. Wiseman (Tyndale, 1982) is more comprehensive than most dictionaries. Its 1300 pages include quantities of information along with excellent maps, charts, diagrams, and an index for cross-referencing.

Unger's Bible Dictionary by Merrill F. Unger (Moody, 1979) is equally good and is available in an inexpensive paperback edition.

The Zondervan Pictorial Encyclopedia edited by Merrill C. Tenney (Zondervan, 1975, 1976) is excellent and exhaustive, and is being revised and updated. However, its five 1000-page volumes are a financial investment, so all but very serious students may prefer to use it at a library.

Unlike a Bible dictionary in the above sense, *Vine's Expository Dictionary of New Testament Words* by W. E. Vine (various publishers) alphabetically lists major words used in the King James Version and defines each New Testament Greek word that KJV translates with that English word. *Vine's* lists verse references where that Greek word appears, so that you can do your own cross-references and word studies without knowing any Greek.

Vine's is a good basic book for beginners, but it is much less complete than other Greek helps for English speakers. More serious students might prefer *The New International Dictionary of New Testament Theology*, edited by Colin Brown (Zondervan) or *The Theological Dictionary of the New Testament* by Gerhard Kittel and Gerhard Friedrich, abridged in one volume by Geoffrey W. Bromiley (Eerdmans).

A *Bible atlas* can be a great aid to understanding what is going on in a book of the Bible and how geography affected events. Here are a few good choices:

The Macmillan Atlas by Yohanan Aharoni and Michael Avi-Yonah (Macmillan, 1968, 1977) contains 264 maps, 89 photos, and 12 graphics. The many maps of individual events portray battles, movements of people, and changing boundaries in detail.

The New Bible Atlas by J. J. Bimson and J. P. Kane (Tyndale, 1985) has 73 maps, 34 photos, and 34 graphics. Its evangelical perspective, concise and helpful text, and excellent research make it a very good choice, but its greatest strength is its outstanding graphics, such as cross-sections of the Dead Sea.

The Bible Mapbook by Simon Jenkins (Lion, 1984) is much shorter and less expensive than most other atlases, so it offers a good first taste of the usefulness of maps. It contains 91 simple maps, very little text, and 20 graphics. Some of the graphics are computer-generated and intriguing.

The Moody Atlas of Bible Lands by Barry J. Beitzel (Moody, 1984) is scholarly, very evangelical, and full of theological text, indexes, and references. This admirable reference work will be too deep and costly for some, but Beitzel shows vividly how God prepared the land of Israel perfectly for the acts of salvation He was going to accomplish in it.

A *handbook* of biblical customs can also be useful. Some good ones are *Today's Handbook of Bible Times and Customs* by William L. Coleman (Bethany, 1984) and the less detailed *Daily Life in Bible Times* (Nelson, 1982).

For Small Group Leaders

How to Lead Small Group Bible Studies (NavPress, 1982).
Just 71 pages. It hits the highlights of how to get members acquainted, ask questions, plan lessons, deal with interpersonal relations, and handle prayer.

The Small Group Leader's Handbook by Steve Barker et al. (InterVarsity, 1982).
Written by an InterVarsity small group with college students primarily in mind. It includes more than the above book on small group dynamics and how to lead in light of them, and many ideas for worship, building community, and outreach. It has a good chapter on doing inductive Bible study.

Getting Together: A Guide for Good Groups by Em Griffin (InterVarsity, 1982).
Applies to all kinds of groups, not just Bible studies. From his own experience, Griffin draws deep insights into why people join groups; how people relate to each other; and principles of leadership, decision making, and discussions. It is fun to read, but its 229 pages will take more time than the above books.

You Can Start a Bible Study Group by Gladys Hunt (Harold Shaw, 1984).
Builds on Hunt's thirty years of experience leading groups. This book is wonderfully focused on God's enabling. It is both clear and applicable for Bible study groups of all kinds.

The Small Group Letter, a special section in *Discipleship Journal* (NavPress).
Unique. Its four pages per issue, six issues per year are packed with practical ideas for asking questions, planning Bible studies, leading discussions, dealing with group dynamics, encouraging spiritual growth, doing outreach, and so on. It stays up to date because writers always discuss what they are currently doing as small group members and leaders. To subscribe, write to Subscription Services, Post Office Box 54470, Boulder, Colorado 80323-4470.

Bible Study Methods

Braga, James. *How to Study the Bible* (Multnomah, 1982).
Clear chapters on a variety of approaches to Bible study: synthetic, geographical, cultural, historical, doctrinal, practical, and so on. Designed to help the ordinary person without seminary training to use these approaches.

Fee, Gordon, and Douglas Stuart. *How to Read the Bible For All Its Worth* (Zondervan, 1982).
After explaining in general what interpretation (exegesis) and application (hermeneutics) are, Fee and Stuart offer chapters on interpreting and applying the different kinds of writing in the Bible: Epistles, Gospels, Old Testament Law, Old Testament narrative, the Prophets, Psalms, Wisdom, and Revelation. Fee and Stuart also suggest good commentaries on each biblical book. They write as evangelical scholars who personally recognize Scripture as God's Word for their daily lives.

Jensen, Irving L. *Independent Bible Study* (Moody, 1963), and *Enjoy Your Bible* (Moody, 1962).
The former is a comprehensive introduction to the inductive Bible study method, especially the use of synthetic charts. The latter is a simpler introduction to the subject.

Wald, Oletta. *The Joy of Discovery in Bible Study* (Augsburg, 1975).
Wald focuses on issues such as how to observe all that is in a text, how to ask questions of a text, how to use grammar and passage structure to see the writer's point, and so on. Very helpful on these subjects.